After my Fall from the Tree House:

a Memoir

Harris Green

authorHOUSE®

AuthorHouse™ LLC
1663 Liberty Drive
Bloomington, IN 47403
www.authorhouse.com
Phone: 1-800-839-8640

Published by AuthorHouse   10/28/2013

ISBN: 978-1-4918-2029-2 (sc)
ISBN: 978-1-4918-2028-5 (e)

Library of Congress Control Number: 2013917596

Table of Contents

Vignettes

Supplement

Parody of a Poem

Letters to the Editor

Non-fiction

Fiction

Dedication

This memoir is dedicated to my wife Annelise Green who, for more than fifty years, has "endured" my "fallen condition" after I fell from the tree house, landed on my head, and became a "free thinker."

Foreword

At not quite three years old, I really did fall from the family tree house and land on my head. Everything I say about the incident has been reported to me by older siblings. What I say about becoming a "free thinker" as a consequence of the fall is of course whimsical, but all of my siblings would agree that my brain works differently, so maybe there is a bit of truth in that speculation.

Acknowledgements

I am of course deeply indebted to my wife Annelise for her patience and hard work as my loving partner. My brothers and sisters have been generous with their reminiscences and suggestions, and they have been good sports about having their secrets revealed. My niece Blair Hawthorne has been tireless in her efforts to create video interviews of each family member and locate old photos. For the section entitled "Remembering Pop Myers," I am indebted to my childhood classmate Sonya Neal Murphree, and to the valuable contacts she gave me: the son and niece of Pop—Dan Myers and Lula Myers Chapman. My neighbor and friend Mike Kupchik has been most generous with his time and expertise as he saw to the digital creation and transmission of the photos to the publisher. Vivian Sheperis, retired English teacher, colleague and friend, performed a masterful job of editing the manuscript and offering valuable suggestions, even to the point of suggesting that I use the 1960 spelling of the Chinese leader, Mao Tse-tung, rather than the more common one today, Mao Zedong. The cover illustration is from the nimble imagination of my friend and neighbor Shirley Ralston.

Note

In most of the vignettes I use the actual names of people and places. I use fictional names where I believe someone might prefer to remain anonymous.

Mama's "Tittybug"

JENNY BEATRICE GREEN (MAMA) GAVE birth eight times and seven of them survived. Each birth involved one or two weeks in the hospital and bed rest after coming home. She lost the baby between my older brother James and me, and she was so grief-stricken she turned James over to my grandparents until she could function. When I was born, in 1938, healthy and sound, she named me Harris Green after Dr. Blue Harris, the obstetrician. I'm glad she didn't name me Blue Green.

Mama nursed me until I was two. I recall climbing up on her lap for "tittybug," maybe flashing a full set of baby teeth. My older sisters say that one day Mama used an old-fashioned weaning technique of putting soot on her nipples. They say that when I got a mouthful of soot, my face screwed up in a frown. I got down from her lap and walked to the bathroom to wet a washcloth. I came back into the bedroom, climbed up on her lap, washed off the soot, and resumed nursing.

My oldest sister Margie told me that when Mama got pregnant with Richard, her last baby, I was still nursing but getting only "blue john." Richard was getting all the good stuff. When Mama realized that she plucked that soothing, nourishing nipple from my toothy mouth and cast me into the harsh, dangerous world of Weaned Humans.

Mama and Harris

The Fall

THE TREE HOUSE WAS IN a chinaberry tree in an area we called "the back field." It was little more than a crude wooden platform bordered by a low railing. My older sisters and brothers were babysitting me and my younger brother, who was in a buggy. I saw a white dog on the ground and leaned over the railing to get a better view. I leaned too far and fell. When I hit the ground, ten feet below, my head struck the edge of a board. My oldest brother Buddy swung down, picked me up, and carried me through the back door into the house. I was bleeding from a wide gash on my forehead. As we passed under the stairway into the entrance hall of the house, I saw Mama, directly above, leaning over the bannister looking down at me.

She put me in the bathtub in a few inches of water to wash off the blood. I thought: *Could getting me clean possibly be more important than fixing my head?* At the hospital they closed the gash with twenty-four stitches, and throughout my childhood whenever we kids told "scar stories" I always told one of the best. Members of my family also enjoyed pushing the hair away from my forehead to show people my impressive scar.

In addition to me, the other children in the tree or the tree house that day were Richard (in his baby buggy), James (eight), Janice (thirteen), Margie (fifteen), George Bliss, Jr. ("Buddy") (eighteen), and a family friend, Edwin Kent (seventeen). Dorothy (ten) was in the house at the time talking to Mama, who was busy at her sewing machine. Dorothy happened to look out the window at the tree house just as I fell. She took a sharp intake of breath, and when Mama asked what was wrong she said, "Nothing."

I learned a few years ago that the intensity of that experience inspired Buddy and Edwin to become doctors. Buddy became an internist, Edwin a surgeon. James and Richard became veterinarians, maybe because they were impressed by the power of that white dog to lure me over the railing. I became a doctor, too, but of the teaching kind . . . maybe because I fell on my head.

the Green Family, Easter morning, 1938

The Green Family's "British Invasion"

SOMETIME IN LATE **1941** OR early 1942, my parents took an interest in the British cadets being trained at Gunter Field on the other side of Montgomery, Alabama. The Royal Air Force had recently defeated the German Luftwaffe in the Battle of Britain but had paid a heavy price in lost pilots. As Winston Churchill said of those brave young men: "Never in the field of human conflict was so much owed by so many to so few."

The Army Air Corps had received a number of British cadets to be trained at Gunter. Mother and Daddy invited several of them to come out to our big country house south of the city. I saw smiling men in blue uniforms, blue caps rakishly worn on the side of the head. They were in our living room with my sisters dancing the jitterbug to Big Band music.

My sisters say that as many as sixty cadets would show up. Mama had put a red light on our big front porch for Christmas and liked it so much she left it up after the holidays. When the cadets called for directions to our house, my naïve sisters would tell them to stop at the house with the red light on the front porch. "No wonder so many of them showed up," they say today.

Margie, sixteen, fell in love with the one named Derek. The emotional intensity of that romance impressed me, a toddler. I learned many years later that Derek, at eighteen, was the squadron commander, and one of his pilots was only fifteen. I recall seeing a photo of the pilots standing next to their Spitfire fighter planes on the runway at Gunter. Each nose section was painted like a shark's head, huge teeth exposed.

James says that one day some of them "buzzed" our house. They flew in from the southwest, as low as possible, hedge-hopping trees as necessary. It being almost dark they hopped over the two-story, Tudor style clubhouse for the Standard Country Club, which bordered our property. A few seconds later, landing lights ablaze, one after the other, they roared over our house, just above the treetops.

Janice and Dorothy were too young for romantic attachments to these daring young men in their flying machines, but they too grew quite fond of them. When the cadets' training ended and departure was nigh, a popular song heard frequently on the radio was "We'll Meet Again." All three of my sisters are in their eighties now, but their eyes still mist up when they recall the sorrow of that separation and the heart-wrenching lyrics: "We'll meet again, don't know where, don't know when. But I know we'll meet again, some sunny day . . . ."

Shortly after their departure, on the night of her high school graduation, Margie heard from Derek, who was en route to England via Canada. He sent her flowers and a Bluebird of Happiness engagement ring. He also sent her a love letter on a phonograph record. In his British accent he spoke lovingly and longingly of his "Vixen." All of the females, including Mama and her girlfriends and my sisters and their girlfriends, cried when listening to the record. Margie and Derek never saw each other again. Several years later both Margie and Janice married WWII American pilots. Today they live together as the widows of those pilots.

Derek and Margie

Mean Mrs. Roosevelt

I WAS ABOUT FIVE WHEN I picked up a magazine, probably *Life*, and saw a full-page, black and white picture of first lady Eleanor Roosevelt and a boy about my age. They were standing in a light rain outside a big, black car with the rear door open. In a black dress and hat, Mrs. Roosevelt was stooped over slightly, looking down at the boy, while smiling her toothy smile. She was holding a closed umbrella over the boy. She had probably just closed it while preparing to get in the car.

In my mind she was about to hit him with the umbrella, and that upset me. I do not remember talking to anybody in the family about it. I just kept it to myself. For some time thereafter I feared and disliked the first lady.

Belt Pride

AT AGE FIVE I WAS very small. For some reason Mama made me wear suspenders, maybe because I had no waist, so a belt had no hips to rest on. I grew to hate suspenders because big boys wore belts. Babies wore suspenders. I don't know how long I pestered her to let me wear a belt, but I will never forget the day I got my first belt.

Our house fronted Woodley Road, which was also U.S. 231. I was so happy to finally get a belt that I wanted the whole world to see me wearing a belt. Since the whole world passed by our house in cars, I ran down the gravel driveway and stopped at the edge of the road so they could see me as they drove past. To make sure they could see the belt I stuck out my skinny stomach as far as I could.

Now, seventy years later, the struggle has returned. I want to wear a belt but I need to wear suspenders. The problem now is *too much* waist. My pants slip below my belly and my pants cuffs slide down over the tops of my shoes. If I could figure out how to wear a belt and keep my pants from sliding down, I would gladly stand by a highway and stick out my stomach so the whole world could see that I'm *not* such a big boy.

Harris in policeman's uniform

Crying in Cloverdale School

I ENTERED FIRST GRADE IN the fall of 1944. I was standing in a dimly lit hallway all alone. I panicked and began crying. I ran down the hallway looking for Dorothy, who had dropped me off in the primary grade section on her way to the junior high section. My teacher, Miss Lamb, chased me down and consoled me. She was kind and gentle. Her left forearm was badly scarred, and that made her even more interesting.

She taught us how to walk quietly in single file. Once in the classroom she had us take a seat at the tiny tables and chairs used by first-graders. I took a seat, but one of the girls, Kitty Sellers, much bigger than I, threw her hip and bumped me out of my chair onto the floor. So I took another chair at another table, next to Ann McKinney.

Soon after we were seated, Miss Lamb gave us crayons and coarse paper with wide lines. She asked us to print our names at the top of the paper. I didn't know what that meant, so when I saw Ann printing A-N-N I copied her name at the top of my paper. Miss Lamb noticed what I did and told me to look up on the blackboard where she printed my name so I could copy it. I don't think any of the other children noticed what she did. Quickly and discreetly she introduced me to the fascinating world of literacy.

Miss Lamb was my teacher for first and second grade. During those war years we learned how to recite the Lord's Prayer and how to sing "The Star Spangled Banner" and "America the Beautiful." We also sang a popular song at the time, "Praise the Lord and Pass the Ammunition." We brought our nickels and dimes to school to put in a paper coin sleeve to save up for buying War Bonds. We also collected newspapers and tin cans to take to school to be turned into war materiel. We flattened the cans by stomping them with our feet.

Our second grade reader was about Alice and Jerry and their dog Spot. The first day I brought it home Richard came running over from the next door neighbor's house to see this fascinating book. I think Miss Lamb had called my parents and told them to listen to me read. My father was the county superintendent for Hill Grocery Company and came home each night quite tired, but somehow he got the job of listening to me read. I sat on the arm of his easy chair and read to him. The adventures of Alice, Jerry and Spot were exciting to me, but one day when I was giving it my all I looked over at Daddy and he was dozing.

White Cowboys and a Red Indian

ONE DAY RICHARD AND BRAD (the boy next door) and I decided to play cowboys and Indians, but we wanted as much realism as possible. As the youngest, Richard was elected to be the Indian. Brad and I put on our cowboy hats and holsters and cap pistols. Then from our cellar we took a can of red paint and two brushes. We stood Richard up against a tree in the backyard and painted him from head to toe, including his short pants and tee shirt.

Soon after we finished, the fumes began burning his eyes and he ran into the house. Mama grabbed him and took him upstairs to the bathroom. She stripped him and used kerosene to get the paint out of his hair and off of every exposed inch of his skin.

Many years later, although the red paint had darkened and much of it had flaked off, it still covered a large section of the tree where Richard had his acting debut as a truly red Indian.

The Day I Burned Up the Golf Course

I WAS SIX OR SEVEN when I decided to run away from home. Life was boring. I longed for high adventure. I packed some tee shirts and short pants in a little cardboard suitcase and put a black, hard-rubber pistol in my pocket. In the living room I found a book of matches I could use for campfires. Behind the house I found a short section of a two by twelve plank to use as a sailing vessel. Plank in one hand and suitcase in the other, I headed through the back field toward the Standard Club golf course.

Soon after I started my adventure Richard came running up. He wanted to join me. I told him, "No, go home!" I climbed the fence and started my trek, but he ran up again, pleading his case. This time I shouted "No!" But he persisted. I reached in my pocket, took out my rubber pistol and hit him on the head. He sat down on a tee box and started crying. I ignored him and continued my adventure.

Off to the left of the fairway in the rough, a field of broom sedge waved in the breeze. About fifty feet wide and a hundred yards long, it ran all the way to the next tee box. Throughout the field were a number of small hills, perhaps added to give golfers an additional challenge for getting out of the rough.

Of course, I didn't know anything about golf. I just knew that hills in this wide open country made great ocean waves to slide down on my "boat." After sliding down a couple of times, I was ready to make a campfire. At the foot of the hill I struck a match and touched it to a stalk of broom sedge. It being the middle of a hot, dry summer, flames immediately surrounded me. I've never been more startled. I tried patting out the flames with my hands, which was utterly useless.

I yelled at Richard, who was still sitting on the golf tee, and he came running. Both of us tried for a few seconds to pat out the flames with our hands but the heat drove us back. Dumbfounded, we stood watching as the prevailing west wind whipped up a conflagration that burned the entire 100-yard section of broom sedge in less than a minute.

14

We didn't wait to see what happened next. We ran home as fast as we could.

We were surprised no one noticed that our hair, eyebrows and eyelashes had been singed and our clothes had a strong smoky odor. Equally surprising, no one was concerned when we both went to bed in the middle of the afternoon, a tactic we used when hoping to avoid a whipping. I was greatly relieved. Richard, however, experienced another emotion.

Although he was only four or five, he displayed a criminal mind. My refusing to take him along, together with my hitting him on the head with my rubber pistol, caused him to seek revenge through blackmail. He told me that if I didn't do what he said he would tell Mama and Daddy that I burned up the golf course.

As I could not imagine a sin greater than burning up a golf course, I agreed. The first order he gave was for us to take sharp kitchen knives and go out to a tree in the side yard even though it was almost dark. We got the knives, climbed up the trunk and straddled two of the biggest branches. There we took our knives and skinned the bark off of the branches until he got tired of that game. For the next few days he made my life miserable. I had to fetch him food and drinks and join in whatever activity suited him. One day when he was feeling especially devilish, he made me take off all my clothes, go outside and run around the house naked.

On about the third or fourth day of his blackmail, I broke his control and felt enormous relief. We had a large chicken house at the junction of the back yard and the back field. We had no chickens at the time, so it made a great playhouse. On that glorious day I walked through the door of the chicken house and caught Richard and Brad sitting on the concrete floor smoking cigarette butts. It was then a matter of "You tell on me and I'll tell on you."

All went well for a day or two, but then we got mad at each other and ran to tell Mama. I yelled, "Richard and Brad were smokin'!!" Richard retaliated with "Harris burned up the golf course!!!" I don't think Mama believed what Richard said, but when Daddy got home, he made us go cut some switches. "And they better be big!" he yelled after us. We both got whipped, but Richard's whipping was worse, probably because his sin was much easier to believe.

Richard and Harris

Janice's False Move

IN 1945 JANICE WAS A senior at Lanier High School. Like so many teenagers that year, she was doing her part for the war effort. Some of the teenage girls danced at the USO with the servicemen, what they called "getting corns for your country." Janice volunteered for the Canteen, which was sponsored by the Junior League and the Red Cross. It was downtown close to Union Station. She and the other girls were supervised by older women who made sure none of the soldiers coming through on the troop trains got overly fresh with the girls, whose job was to run across the tracks with coffee, donuts, cigarettes, chewing gum, sandwiches and magazines and hand them through the windows to the troops.

One day two Army Air Corps cadets stationed at Maxwell Field came to the canteen on a motorcycle. Janice chatted with them, and when she left to go home they followed her. When she arrived home she invited them in to meet our parents.

Soon after the introductions were made, Janice and the cadets went in the living room to dance the jitterbug. That morning Janice had borrowed Margie's false breasts ("falsies) to augment her feminine charm.

The canteen uniform the girls wore was modestly loose and Janice weighed only about a hundred pounds at the time, so while she was jitterbugging all over the living room floor, she felt something moving and suddenly the falsies fell out of the bottom of her dress and hit the floor. Without missing a beat of the music, she swept up the falsies and ran into kitchen.

She told Mama she couldn't go back to the living room, but Mama said she must, so she walked back in holding two glasses of iced water while feeling "quite deflated."

As a widow in her seventies, Janice told this story in one of the scenes of a play I co-wrote to honor the World War Two generation. Her story got the biggest laugh. The audiences loved it. She told hundreds of theater patrons about this incident in her youth but never told Dan, the late husband she was married to for forty-four years.

Janice and Margie stifling Harris

Dancing Bloomers

EVEN THOUGH RICHARD AND I had our squabbles, we were occasionally co-conspirators as when we agreed that adults were much too formal and stiff when they visited each other. Our parents' good friends the Todds were coming over for a visit, and when they arrived, Mama and Daddy invited them into our living room where they all sat and talked. Richard and I decided it would be funny to disturb the stiff formality of that scene by doing something outrageous.

We got Daddy's rod and reel and attached a pair of "bloomers" (underwear) to the fish hook. While I stood next to the staircase railing upstairs holding the rod, Richard pulled extra line off the reel as he walked down the stairs with the bloomers. At the bottom of the stairs, he crouched against the wall next to the open double French doors. Without revealing himself he threw the bloomers across the living room, close to where the adults were sitting. As he ran back upstairs I began slowly reeling the bloomers across the floor, giving them an occasional jerk.

We didn't think about the consequences of our behavior. It just seemed like a great joke. Either the adults didn't see the dancing bloomers or enjoyed the joke with us. The fact that we heard no reaction from the adults didn't dampen our enjoyment. We giggled as quietly as we could. Maybe they concurred that a little levity made the visit more enjoyable.

Living with an "Angel"

WHEN MAMA TURNED JAMES OVER to our grandparents, the country was in the depths of the Depression. Granddaddy was out of work, and he and Granny were living with us. It wasn't long before James became "Angel," which they called him for the rest of their lives. Over the years, the rest of the family decided that "Angel" might not accurately describe James. Margie reports that one day after she had prepared a relaxing bath containing bath salts, she entered the family's only bathroom and found a large snapping turtle swimming in the bathtub. James had caught it in a farm pond earlier that day and noticed its skin was drying out. Margie expressed little concern for the condition of the turtle's skin.

At times I was a less-than-angelic co-conspirator. One day James and I decided it would be fun to put a "bull's eye on Richard's butt" by setting him on a burner on Mama's electric stove. We put him in a woven wood-strip peach basket and set him on the burner. He was too little to get down, so he squirmed and fussed as the burner got redder. Soon we began smelling the burning wood and decided he was done, so we lifted him down. We saw no bull's eye and there was no harm done to his tiny butt.

One evening while I was struggling with the third grade fraction problems Miss Lide had assigned, James, in eighth grade, took over and did my homework so I could go with him to his friend's house down the road. He and Joe had planned a bow and arrow fight in the living room.

Apparently the adults had gone for the evening because they would never have approved of what we did. I recall us turning out all the lights and shooting at each other from behind the furniture. The archery equipment was all homemade out of tree branches and string, so it wasn't strong, but one of us could have been hit in the eye.

Fighting in the dark reminds me of when we had billy club fights in the dark using rolled-up newspapers or magazines. On those rare occasions when the parents of one of us boys would not be home after dark, we gathered at that house with our "clubs." We pulled down all the shades and turned out all the lights. When the signal was given we began swatting each other in the dark while stumbling all over the house looking for each other. The best of those fights, and also my last, occurred when one of my buddies and I were sixteen. We were at his house at night with his sister and her friend, both seventeen. We challenged them to a fight in the dark, and I never had so much fun getting hit while pushing off my assailant.

On another occasion, when I was about eight, James and Joe challenged Brad and me to a slingshot battle using hard, green chinaberries. There was an old "servants quarters" in our back yard, consisting of a single-car garage with a dirt floor and an upstairs apartment with three rooms. It was so old and dilapidated that it would soon be torn down, but until that day we children enjoyed playing in it.

James and Joe took the old house and would shoot out of the bedroom window upstairs. Brad and I were given a standard cardboard box we could "hide" behind in the middle of the lawn. Within the first minute of the so-called battle, our box had multiple dents and a few holes, and we were getting hit on any exposed body part. Brad and I soon abandoned the worthless box and ran the other way.

Granddaddy gave us silver dollars for our birthdays. On my eighth birthday I received three silver dollars. One day James and his pal Freddy were in need of money, so they came to see me. James told me what a big boy I was getting to be. In fact, he continued, I am now old enough to lend money. That information made me feel like a really big boy, so when he gave me permission to lend him my three silver dollars, I gladly handed them over. That was in the summer of 1946. Given normal interest charges on personal loans since then, he owes me a fortune, but today he pleads ignorance of the loan.

Harris in fourth grade

My Best Christmas Ever

CHRISTMAS OF 1947, WHEN I was nine, is the best Christmas I've ever had. I was just young enough to make my parents and older siblings believe that I still believed in Santa Claus. To be more convincing, I wrote the obligatory letter to Santa and listened to the big radio in the living room when Santa read letters from children.

In my letter I asked for a new cowboy hat, a new cap pistol with holster and several rolls of caps. I also asked for an archery set with real target arrows and a Daisy pump BB rifle. Richard, seven, asked for the same things. A final gift we asked for jointly was a pony, which we knew was a very long shot.

One of our Christmas traditions was to get the biggest Christmas tree Daddy could find at one of the grocery stores he supervised. The only kind of tree available was the native cedar. Our house had a large entrance hall in which the stairway wound around the back wall up to the second floor. The space within the stairwell is where we put the tree, which was typically so tall that we had to go up to the second floor to place the star on top.

As the family did every year, that Christmas we lined up on the staircase according to age, youngest to oldest, to go down to the living room in single file. At the front was Richard, then me, James, Dorothy, Janice, Margie, Buddy, Mama, and Daddy.

When I saw the cowboy outfit and BB gun and archery set I was thrilled. Just when I thought I couldn't get more excited, somebody told me and Richard to see what Santa left outside. We ran out and saw a pony ready to ride. At that point I was delirious. Richard and I rode the pony around the yard together then separately, until we had to come into the house.

Having a pony as a Christmas present meant that Christmas would last longer than usual. The back field was about an acre in size, so we had plenty of pasture for Madam, slightly swaybacked and chestnut in color. I found out later that she was twelve years old, so "Madam" was a fitting name. She couldn't have been more gentle and patient as she entertained not only the neighborhood children but also those at church picnics.

Early one Sunday morning in the early spring, I was playing with Brad, who had also gotten a pony for Christmas. We were sitting on the fence between our back fields. I looked over at Madam, who was restfully grazing after a strenuous Saturday carrying children around the church grounds. Then I noticed four black legs between her four chestnut legs. At first I thought it was a dog, but then Madam turned and I saw it was a colt.

I ran back to the house and yelled, "Madam has a colt!" Some of them barely dressed, the whole family ran out the back door into the field and discovered a coal black colt barely able to stand. He seemed to be all legs as he tried to keep his balance. His blackness was relieved by a white blaze on his forehead and large, blue eyes. My sister Margie was so attracted to him that she got too close and Madam drew her foot back and kicked her in the thigh. The next day her whole thigh was black and blue.

A few weeks later, Daddy sold Madam and her colt. He made it clear to me and Richard that we were only a house with a big yard, not a farm. He convinced us that the colt would be much happier on a farm pasture with plenty of space to run and play, a sentiment Richard and I could fully understand.

the Green family, Christmas morning, 1955

A Very Brief Encounter
with the Three Stooges

ONE DAY SHORTLY BEFORE WE discovered Madam was pregnant, Richard and I were in the chicken house/stable watching her eat. Not knowing she had recently fallen and torn her shoulder muscle, Richard patted her on that muscle and she "in a blur" jerked her head up and bit his nose. Fortunately, Richard was knocked backward by the blow. Otherwise, she might have bitten off his nose.

Daddy happened to be home at the time, so he called for an appointment with our pediatrician, Dr. Mars. I went downtown with Richard and Daddy, and after the doctor treated his nose and gave him a tetanus shot, Daddy agreed to let us stay in town and go to a movie. A Three Stooges film was showing at the Charles Theater, so he dropped us off with enough money for a ticket, candy and a bus ride home. As children we never bothered arriving at the start of a film. We would just arrive, watch the rest of the "picture show," and then watch the beginning up to the point where we came in.

The rest of the story is mostly a blur in my memory, but what I recall is entering the theater, seeing somebody onstage talking, then everybody going out to the lobby. I decided the movie was over for the day and took Richard with me out to the lobby. There I saw Stooge "Larry" signing autographs. The Three Stooges were there in person for some kind of Three Stooges Festival.

I guess the crowd and hullabaloo bothered me, so I took Richard out of the theater. For some reason we no longer had any money. Maybe the cost of the tickets had taken all we had. Richard claims I gave the rest of our money to a panhandler. Whatever the cause, we had no money, and I decided we would walk the four miles home from downtown. The trip required several street changes, but we had no trouble and arrived back a couple of hours later. No one at home seemed surprised by our adventure. It was just another day at the Green house.

Fore!

SOMETIMES WHEN I WAS PLAYING on the Standard Club golf course I would see golfers and watch closely what they were doing. Only eight or nine at the time, I knew nothing about the game and learned strictly by observation. The first lesson I noted was to keep the left arm straight. On two or three occasions I found a golf club and just kept it. It didn't seem like stealing to me. I kept the golf balls I found. Why not golf clubs?

I practiced what I learned but didn't get serious until I was sixteen. That year my friends and I began practicing our own techniques. None of us got any lessons. Later that year Montgomery got its first municipal golf course, Elsmeade, only a few miles away. We had an opportunity to play golf legally although we never thought that playing the Standard Club course was illegal since the members rarely played.

Each of us worked odd or part-time jobs, so we had money to pay greens fees and buy used clubs out of the pro's barrel. We learned that we only needed the even or odd numbered clubs, so over time, at $5 each, I bought a 2-wood, 3, 5, 7, 9 irons and a putter. I still have the putter, which is a duplicate of Bobby Jones' Calamity Jane with its hickory shaft and leather grip. I learned recently that it might fetch a couple of hundred dollars on E-bay.

One day when I was playing there by myself, I came to the second tee box and had a strange experience. Bordering the golf course was Allenport, the municipal airport for private planes. The landing pattern for the planes was directly over the second tee. The planes would land maybe 200 feet behind the tee. We were sort of used to seeing the planes coming in for a landing, but on this day (maybe because I was concentrating so hard on my swing) I didn't see how close a Piper Cub was when I swung. Unfortunately, the ball went higher than usual and when I looked up it was heading straight for the Piper's windshield. The plane suddenly dipped, the ball flew over the cockpit, and the plane rose and glided in for a landing.

The following summer Elsmeade staged a junior tournament. My buddies and I were put in the second flight. Each match was nine-hole stroke play. I beat a couple of my buddies to make it to the championship. When I saw I would play a nine-year-old boy, I was confident of victory. That's when I learned that a drive of 150 yards down the middle is much better than one of 225 yards into the woods. I also witnessed much better putting. Humbled by defeat but proud of my second place finish, I took my trophy home to show my family. My mother said, "I didn't know you played golf!"

For the next twenty-five years I played very little golf, but once I finished college and had a full-time job, I took it up seriously. I started changing my golf swing and buying better equipment, but I shouldn't have because my golf game has never been as good as it was when I played by the seat of my pants with five-dollar clubs.

Learning English the Hard Way

IN THE FIFTH GRADE WITH Mrs. Davis, I had an embarrassing experience in which I learned a new word. One day after we returned from our restroom break, the restroom monitor reported to the teacher and the whole class that Harris had *urinated* on the floor. I was impressed by that big word that meant *peeing*. I didn't do it on purpose. I was still too small to get a proper trajectory into the urinal.

My sixth grade teacher, Miss Cox, and I were walking to the lunchroom together. She was a tall, imposing figure, so I had to scurry to keep up with her. As we walked she was telling me that we should use *an* before vowels, as in *an apple,* and *a* before consonants, as in *a pear.* She smiled indulgently when I told her, quite sincerely, that I didn't think my brain could hold any more knowledge.

In my seventh grade English class, I was most impressed by Jo Ann Scarborough who, when asked a question by our teacher, Miss Stough, replied "mentally or physically?" That level of sophistication was completely alien to me. I was jealous. Jo Ann's father was a teacher at the high school, which helped account for her erudition. She went on to become a teacher herself.

Junior High Jackasses

AT SUMMER CAMP BEFORE BEGINNING junior high in September, I signed up for boxing. Because I was less than five feet tall and weighed seventy pounds, I was put in the flyweight division. When school started, maybe because of my small size, a few of the junior high girls considered me cute, so I learned to deal with cuteness and going on "dates." By the eighth grade some of my buddies were coping with puberty and acting like jackasses, which meant that pre-pubescent me had to do the same to be accepted.

One such hormone-driven activity we engaged in for a short time was what we called "Tomming," a name derived from "Peeping Tom." We prowled the neighborhood at night looking to see naked girls and women through bedroom and bathroom windows. We never saw anything noteworthy. Other boys claimed to have seen much more than we did, but I found their stories hard to believe. When we learned that "tomming" was a serious crime, we stopped.

In the early fifties in Alabama, corporal punishment was common practice, but the younger generations today cannot understand how, for us jackasses, it was barely "corporal" or "punishment." When I got out of line, I sometimes got paddled, but I understood that my punishment was for my own good. Of course I didn't like it, but I always knew I deserved it. One of the disciplinarians at Cloverdale was Coach Sellers, who used a wooden baseball bat cut lengthwise to give it a flat side. He used it to deliver a whack that would lift me off the floor—but mainly because I jumped as he swung.

He depended more on humiliation and dread than pain. One day he told me to be in his classroom at the start of the next period. When I got there he told me to lean over the front of his desk with my rump facing his class of eighth grade science students. After strolling about the room twirling his half baseball bat, sonorously detailing the transgressions of "Mr. Green," he took his position, faked a couple of swings, and then gave me a whack.

30

I think all of us boys admired Coach Sellers in part <u>because</u> of the paddling. It made us feel manly, and since we knew we deserved the punishment it was swift justice. And our parents weren't told, which could have led to more punishment when we got home. Back then parents and teachers joined forces to civilize the heathens. Lawyers weren't lurking around every corner to provide "justice" for the parents and child.

Soon after retiring in 1995, I made a trip back to Cloverdale to see what changes had occurred since I had graduated in 1953. In the early fifties the shop teacher Miss Kirkland looked more like a large man than a woman. She paddled us boys with thin, flat strips of wood. That day in 1995, the shop teacher was a very pretty young woman who kept order by threatening the students with a cellphone call to their parents. In the fifties, the principal, Mr. Taylor, maintained order by simply strolling up and down the corridors during class breaks. Any miscreant who disrupted class would sit in his office for the rest of the period and might feel his paddle before he left. That day in 1995 uniformed policemen patrolled the halls of Cloverdale School.

Christmas Greenbacks

AT SOME POINT IN THE late forties or early fifties we boys discovered an easy way to make Christmas present money. A very large woodlot nearby was our source of Christmas greenery we could sell door to door.

Abundant longleaf pine saplings provided pine boughs. The occasional holly bush spray nicely complemented the pine with dark green, thorny leaves and red berries. In the middle of the woods was a thirty-foot high magnolia tree. We climbed along its massive limbs and cut the best-looking, dark green leaves. We painted some of those leaves silver or gold.

The Holy Grail of Christmas greenery was a very large clump of mistletoe loaded with white berries that would not fall off when the clump was removed. A single, leafless, deciduous tree might have as many as five or six clumps of mistletoe. But all of them were high in the tree.

Some boys would shoot the main stem of the clump with a .22 rifle, causing the mistletoe to fall to the ground, but as it fell many of the delicate, white berries were knocked off. We took a pocketknife and climbed up to the clump, carefully cut it away from the tree and gingerly carried it down.

When we had enough cardboard boxes loaded with our greenery, we walked house to house selling our crop. A pine bough would bring in maybe a dime. For a few dark green magnolia leaves, maybe fifteen cents. We soon learned that the gold or silver ones didn't sell as well and quit painting them. The holly and the mistletoe brought in the most money. Each spray or clump could be worth as much as seventy-five cents.

After two or three days of hunting and selling, I could raise as much as four or five dollars, which was enough to buy presents at Woolworth's for my parents and six brothers and sisters.

Remembering Pop Myers

DURING THE YEARS I WAS a student at Cloverdale, I walked home by crossing the campus of Huntingdon College. On a small patch of land at the edge of the school athletic field and across the street from the college campus was Pop Myers' popcorn stand. His main customers were the college students and the children at Cloverdale.

Today I consider him an icon of a cherished, bygone era. He was Walter Jerome Myers, known to us children as Pop. Born in 1879, he represents a time when love of God and service to others was more important than the bottom line. It was a time when concern for children was driven by their welfare rather than by fear of lawsuit.

"Myers Pop Corn" and "Pop's" in bold red paint against the stark white paint adorned the sides of his tiny stand. Pop's was an ideal location for selling soft drinks, popcorn, and candy bars, each costing five cents. The stand was maybe eight feet by ten feet, just large enough for a double drink cooler, a popcorn machine, a small refrigerator and one stool.

As I recall, the stand looked something like a trolley car. Two long, wooden benches on opposite sides of the stand invited us kids to linger and socialize in the shade of the chinaberry tree. It was a popular hang-out with lots of children of all ages, but I don't recall any conflicts— no name calling, no scuffling in the well-trod dust surrounding the stand. We were too busy enjoying our treats and each other, under the ever watchful eye of the old man. He never had to correct us. We just understood how to behave at Pop's.

I associate Pop with the color white. He wore white pants and a white dress shirt with black bow tie, a white cotton cap and a full-length white cotton apron. He sold wonderful, snow-white popcorn (no butter) in small white bags, and frozen Baby Ruths and Butterfingers.

I cherish my memory of his "shake-ice" soft drinks. We didn't call them soft drinks or soda pop. Everything was a "co cola," even if it wasn't. In addition to Coca Cola, we could get Pepsi Cola ("twelve full ounces, that's a lot!"), RC Cola, Dr. Pepper, Grape Cola, Nehi Orange,

7-Up and, strangest of all, Buffalo Rock, which I guess contained carbonated water, lots of ginger, and some mystery ingredients. But the best "shake-ice" drink was the only Coca Cola product available: what is now called "Classic Coke" in the famous six-ounce, curvaceous bottle.

Pop made the shake-ice drinks by putting the bottles next to great chunks of dry ice in his cooler. He closely watched them, and just before the liquid became icy enough to dislodge the cap, he would take it out and give it to a customer, along with a straightened coat hanger with a loop in the end. This was used to dig down into the ice and drag out the delectable ice chunks. I suppose today's equivalent would be the "slushy" ice products available at convenience stores, but I can't help but think ours tasted better since we had to work for it. The devices were called "juker wires," and we delighted in digging down into the bottle and dragging the frosty morsels into our mouths.

Pop's younger brother M.B. "Pop" Myers operated the same kind of stand at the entrance to Oak Park, about two miles north. On the sign was the slogan, "By my corn I shall be known." The older Pop's son Pop, Jr. and his wife Tut sometimes worked for their uncle at the Oak Park stand. They could be seen driving their pickup truck down Forest Avenue in front of the park with their dog standing on the hood like some huge ornament. Junior placed a mat on the hood so the dog could get his footing and strapped him in a harness to hold him in place.

Soon after Pop's wife died in 1967, Pop died. He had operated his stand since 1922 and had befriended hundreds of children whose school pictures covered the walls of his tiny stand. He had also sent and received hundreds of post cards and Christmas cards. Even though he had only a third grade education, Pop loved poetry and filled up a few school notebooks with his verse, probably between visits from us children. One of my favorites is: "We live best when we are gone/In the lives of others that still live on."

Very soon after he abandoned his stand, the city rushed in and removed it. But Pop's legacy is much greater than wood, tin, school pictures and juker wires. At the spot where his stand once stood, the city should erect a marble statue of Pop to honor a man who epitomized an era.

It was a time when "Yes, ma'am" and "No, sir" easily rolled off a tongue sweetened by a frozen Snickers bar, or soured by Octagon soap if it got "dirty." It was a time when children were strictly regulated at school but strictly NOT regulated out of school. We could go anywhere and feel safe because we were supervised by every adult who saw or heard us. There was no such thing as parents "not getting involved."

Because we were safe, our stay-at-home mothers didn't worry about us. We walked, rode our bikes, or took the bus. The city pool had two diving boards and a ten-foot high dive platform because the city didn't have to worry about a lawsuit if someone got hurt. You used them at your own risk. After riding our bicycles across town to get to the park we would spend all day playing in the pool. The exercise we got kept us physically fit. Today, overweight parents chauffer their overweight children, making the dense traffic too dangerous for bycycle riding.

If Pop tried to operate his stand today, he would have to meet a strict building code that would have destroyed the charm of the old one. The rickety stand stood less than ten feet from a busy street (Fairview Avenue), and after school it was surrounded by dozens of kids. City attorneys today would have apoplexy. And I won't even go into his practice of giving children metal rods to stick in their mouths, to say nothing about what certain journalists and politicians would say about an old man who surrounded himself with children.

In Pop's world, life was simple. If we had a nickel, we stopped by and had a treat. If not, we kept walking, or riding our bicycles. Maybe we could find a ripe persimmon or some wild plums. There was a persimmon tree on the college campus, and thickets of wild plums were fairly common along fence lines. We were healthy, and our problems were few. Having a nickel or two just made a good life better. To me, Pop's was a wonderland of snow-white popcorn, frozen Baby Ruths, juker wires, shake-ice "co colas" and not a care in the world.

Margie's Condom Balloons

A FEW YEARS AGO MARGIE got up the nerve to tell us about an incident that occurred when she and George were dating. They met when George was a B-24 pilot during WWII. He was stationed at Maxwell Field, and they met in downtown Montgomery.

One day Margie and George double-dated with Margie's girlfriend Cecile Todd and her beau Tom Lightbody. While they were riding around the city, Margie started rummaging through the glove compartment looking for a map. She discovered a box of condoms, "a full box" she likes to emphasize. She pretended not to know what they were and asked George if they were balloons, but he only stammered. She took one out, blew it up, reached out the passenger side window, and tied it to his radio antenna. Then she took another and another and did the same.

Margie said that both men were embarrassed and tongue-tied while she and Cecile struggled to stifle their giggles. I guess George must have admired Margie's spunk because they continued to date until he was sent to England to fly bombing runs over Germany. After the war George returned to his home in Detroit, but a couple of years later he called and asked to see her again. He came down in his wine-colored Hudson convertible and contiued their courtship. They were married in September, 1949.

The First Time I Saw TV

IN THE SUMMER OF 1951 I turned thirteen. Margie and George lived in Birmingham, which had two television stations. Montgomery had none. Margie and George were visiting Mama and Daddy, and when it was time for them to drive back to Birmingham on Sunday night Margie asked if I would like to go home with them for a visit.

I was packed and ready to go in just a few minutes because I was thrilled at the prospect of seeing TV for the first time. I had heard wonderful reports about the programs but nobody I knew had a set. We left at about 8:00 p.m. for what was then a three-hour drive. In the back of George's ford convertible I was so excited I could hardly sit still. We rolled along U.S. 31 through towns named Pratville, Clanton, Thorsby and Alabaster.

Finally we came down Red Mountain by the colossal statue of Vulcan and could see the city lights spread out below. The smell of the coal-fired furnaces in the steel mills confirmed that this was indeed Birmingham and I would soon be watching television. After another twenty minutes of driving through the city, we pulled into the parking space in front of their modest apartment.

I jumped out of the car, ran up to the door and squirmed with excitement while George unlocked the door. He then strolled over to the television set and clicked it on. After a thirty-second warm-up, with me down on my knees two feet away, straining my eyes, a fuzzy image of a waving American flag appeared, and from the speaker came: "Oh oh say can you see, by the dawn's early light . . . ." The next thing I saw was a test pattern. The broadcast day had ended.

Uninvited Swimming Pool Guests

DURING MY EARLY TEENS MY best buddy was Emory Erb, a classmate at Cloverdale School who lived down the road. Emory and I were free spirits who were not aware of some of the common courtesies. Among the more prominent families in Montgomery were the Pattersons, two brothers who owned the most popular flower shop in the city.

One of the brothers lived on an estate four miles out in the country. We learned that he had a swimming pool with diving board, the only private pool we'd ever heard about. Perhaps because we couldn't grasp the concept of a private pool, we decided that nobody would mind if we enjoyed the pool also. On more than one occasion on a hot summer's day, Emory and I walked the four miles to the estate. Barefooted, wearing only swim trunks and carrying a towel, we strolled up the long, uphill driveway to the back of the house and jumped in the pool.

Since we were convinced they wouldn't mind us being there, we saw no need to be quiet. In fact, we made more noise than normal because we were competing to see which one of us would be first to learn how to do one and a half flips off of the diving board. After frolicking for a half-hour or so, we dried off and stopped by their scuppernong grape arbor in the side yard for a few grapes to eat on our way home.

Thirty years later at our twenty-fifth high school reunion, one of Mr. Patterson's daughters, Jane, who had been a classmate throughout grade school, told us that on one of our trips she saw us playing in the pool and wanted to go out to talk to us but her mother made her stay in the house. We apologizeed for our rudeness but smiled. She smiled, too.

A Racist Escapade

IN THE SUMMER OF 1952, I discovered I was a racist. Before that unforgettable summer night, I believed that racial discrimination was as natural as the sunrise. People with dark skin worked for people with light skin, and they lived in another part of town. We were to "mind" black adults but not give them the same respect we gave white adults. For example, we called them "Beulah" or "Willie."

For us, black middle class citizens didn't exist. We had no contact with black businessmen, teachers, doctors, ministers. All black people we saw were illiterate or nearly so. They took the city bus to their jobs working for white people as "maids" or "yard men," often walking a long way between the bus stop and the house. Occasionally we would see an old black man in overalls driving a weather-beaten, mule-drawn wagon to or from his shack in the country. I never saw a black person driving a car.

One especially hot day we decided to sleep out that night on the Standard Club golf course. The temperature at night in that wide open space was not just cool; it was cold, which was a welcome opportunity to sleep under a blanket in those days before air-conditioned houses. We discussed what to do that night and decided we would go "coon busting" in black sections of town, a popular pastime among white adolescent boys that summer. We rode three motorbikes, two to a bike, with each boy on back carrying two water balloons. We filled our balloons at gas stations.

Our first target was a half-dozen small black children playing in cardboard boxes in the front yard of their apartment building. As each motorbike passed them, the boy in back lobbed a water balloon at the children. We got exactly the reaction we wanted. By the time the third bike reached them, the children had the boxes on their heads.

We then picked promising targets on both sides of the street. Mine was a middle-aged black woman waiting for a bus. She was wearing a nice white dress. She looked like she might be going to choir practice. I hit her with a balloon. She sprang backwards and her mouth flew open. I could hear her shouting as we sped away.

In front of us we saw a young, well-dressed black man running down the street toward Jim and Brit who were waiting for a traffic light to change. We started screaming to get their attention. When they finally heard us and turned around, the young man was no more than fifty feet from them, so they ran the red light and got away. We sped by the wet, angry man and caught up with Jim and Brit.

Our last sortie that night took us to a black neighborhood in the oldest section of the city. We were riding along a dimly lit street going up a hill when I saw an old black man in shabby clothes shuffling along. As we passed him I lobbed a water balloon at him, and it broke over his upper back and shoulders. When I looked back he had not reacted at all. He just kept his head down and kept walking.

I was the one who reacted. I was shocked. This old man was so used to insults and abuse that he didn't even respond to them. His dignity in defiance of my juvenile disrespect made me deeply ashamed. I was a punk.

On our way back to the golf course, we rode down Dartmouth Circle directly onto a fairway of the course, over a low rise and down to where we planned to sleep. After parking the motorbikes behind a large bank of wild privet shrubs at the edge of the fairway, we took our blankets across the fairway to a green, about a hundred yards from the street. We were joking and jostling each other while getting settled down for the night when Ralph saw the sky above the rise light up. He alerted us then ran over to the edge of the privet and crept up the rise to a point where he could look down on the source of the light.

He looked at the scene for a few seconds then ran back to us. Breathless, he reported seeing Mr. Phelps standing next to his car, wearing his customary brown felt fedora. He also saw four policemen standing alongside two squad cars. We all knew Mr. Phelps as a police detective who also worked for the *Alabama Journal*, Montgomery's evening newspaper. His job was to bring the papers to a distribution center where we picked them up to deliver on our routes.

We had no clue as to what we could have done to alert the police, but we wasted no time getting out of there. We grabbed our blankets and ran toward a narrow strip of broom sedge grass. On the other side of the strip was a barbed wire fence that we climbed then jumped into a pasture of Johnson grass. We bounded along for about forty feet then lay down. Almost immediately one of the squad cars appeared across the fence, the car's spotlight sweeping over the grass we were lying in. After it passed by, we jumped up and bounded in the opposite direction toward home.

By the next day, our only explanation for the police activity was somebody reporting us as trespassers on the golf course. As we were walking back to where we had hidden our motorbikes, we saw a group of golfers. They saw us going behind the bank of privet shrubs and one of them came over to interrogate us. He found out we were the ones the police were looking for. He was an official at the club and had been notified the night before. We found out from him what caused all the excitement.

The night before, when we came back from our raid, the woman who lived in the house that bordered the fairway called the police. She told them that three motorcycles had roared past her house and onto the golf course. She saw three boys with a girl riding behind each boy. At first we thought we were in big trouble, but after we assured him there were no girls involved, he just gave us a good scolding and sent us on our way.

That experience taught me that boys and girls having a spend-the-night party on the golf course is much worse than just boys spending the night. We were afraid that since he had taken our names Mr. Phelps would be notified, but he wasn't. It never occurred to us that the police might have come because "colored" people had reported six white boys on three motorcycles riding through their neighborhood hitting men, women, children—even old men—with water balloons. Maybe they did call to complain but got no satisfaction from the all-white, all-male police department.

My Prophecy to be a Postman

AT THE END OF THE ninth grade, I finished all of my coursework at Cloverdale except for attending summer school to repeat Algebra I. Since we would be moving to Lanier High in the fall, Cloverdale staged a graduation. Part of the ceremony included a kind of "prophecy" event in which each of us would get our "fortune" told. All of the most popular students got prophecies that envisioned them as industrialists, super athletes, movie stars, famous scientists, and so forth. My fortune showed that I would be delivering mail. After hearing about all that citizen royalty, I was quite disappointed that my fate did not include an exalted position in society.

Sweet Romance

ATTENDING CLASS ON MY FIRST day at Lanier High School contrasted sharply with that terrifying day when I raced through the halls of Cloverdale looking for my sister. For one thing, high school started with the tenth grade, so as a sophomore I was older than freshmen at other high schools in other cities. Still, at just over five feet in height and weighing less than ninety pounds, I was intimidated by the big upperclassmen. At the start of the eleventh grade I was 5'4" and weighed less than a hundred pounds. Over the next year I grew to 5'11" and weighed about 130. I went from a "shrimp" to a "beanpole."

Along with the growth spurt came puberty. In the summer of 1954 I became infatuated with a girl my age who worked in Kress department store downtown. Although I talked to her, briefly, only once or twice, I recall her being round and curvy and probably soft and warm. And she smelled good. I had done some smooching with neighborhood girls as far back as age fourteen, but this girl was a woman. When I thought about her while walking somewhere, I felt like I was floating above the ground. I fell in love with love. I couldn't get enough of the romantic songs of that summer. Today, when I hear the theme song from "The High and the Mighty" or "Three Coins in the Fountain," it's once again 1954 and love is in the air.

The Christmas Tree Fort

DURING THE AFTER-CHRISTMAS BLAHS, WHEN the world seems depressed, I am cheered by the sight of a discarded Christmas tree on the curb. For most people, such a scene makes them even more depressed, recalling the tree's recent splendor at the heart of family life. But I remember when my boyhood friends and I gave the trees a second life as breastworks in our Christmas tree forts.

Between Christmas and New Year's we would go from house to house collecting discarded Christmas trees. We would drag them to the field in back of our house to a clearing under a large mulberry tree. In the summer, with all the bushes and trees leafed out, the area made a splendid fort. We whiled away the hours talking, reading comic books, and choking on cigarette smoke. Sometimes we climbed up into the tree and ate the mulberries, which looked like small blackberries, but the juice was sweeter, and it stained our skin and clothes. A lot of the fruit fell to the ground and covered the floor of our fort, so for most of the summer we could have been known as "the purple feet gang."

Not fifty feet from the mulberry was the chinaberry tree where we stocked up on chinaberries for the slingshot battles we fought in defense of our fort. The hard, green berries made excellent ammo and, despite their bitter taste, we crammed our cheeks full of berries and spit them one by one into the pockets of our slingshots for rapid firepower.

In the winter, the Christmas trees took the place of the natural vegetation, but of course we had no chinaberries. So we had to resort to other weapons. Everybody had fireworks left over from New Year's Eve. We made full use of them in our wintertime conflicts. Roman candles became bazookas, sparklers became signaling devices, and zebras (firecrackers) became the propellant for pipe guns that shot mud. Zebras also made an excellent explosive for mud grenades. We had enough sense not to use the really dangerous fireworks like cherry bombs or ash cans. The nice thing about cherry bombs is that you could flush them down the toilet at school and the fuse would stay lit. When

45

it exploded along the sewer line, the roar reverberated throughout the bowels of the school.

The Christmas tree fort battle I remember most occurred when I was sixteen and really too old to be playing. The younger kids in the neighborhood had made a Christmas tree fort around the mulberry tree and were getting ready for battle. My friend Freddie and I decided to take on both armies.

A half dozen boys were in the fort, including Richard. While most of us Greens had been small as young children, Richard was the smallest. Consequently, he felt more comfortable with younger children. By the time of this battle, Richard was fourteen and the youngest was about nine. Freddie and I had several zebras and lots of mud at our disposal, so we decided to get the battle underway with a little mortar fire. We were standing close to the chinaberry tree, and I took a fresh zebra and molded it inside a mud ball, leaving the fuse sticking out of the top. I cocked my arm behind my head, where Freddie was waiting with a burning match to light the fuse. As soon as the fuse was well lit I lobbed the mortar shell high into the leafless branches of the mulberry tree. It bounced around among the branches before going off in a shattering blast just over their heads. To lend authenticity to the launch, Freddie and I made whistling sounds to simulate the effect of an incoming round.

The boys put up a feeble defense with their roman candles and firecrackers but all in vain. As the third or fourth mortar exploded, stinging them with bits of mud and sand, they panicked and ran in all directions out of the fort, heading for home. With the acrid smell of gunpowder smoke drifting in the air, Freddie and I slapped each other on the back, congratulating ourselves for a swift victory.

Later, while strolling down the road to Freddie's house, we decided that victory had come too quickly. With heavy hearts, we realized that our days as Christmas tree fort warriors were over. After a short period of reflective silence, we began fantasizing out loud about a girl at school, known to us teenage boys as "Sara Jean, The Love Machine."

An Unused Teachable Moment

IN THE FALL OF 1955 in Montgomery the only "social issues" discussed were what the debutantes would wear to the various "coming out" balls. World War Two had been decisively won, America was the undisputed leader of the free world, and we had fallen into the very comfortable and complacent "Eisenhower Trance." The lingering effects of the McCarthy era in Alabama meant that pink politics was bad but pink skin was good. However, on December 1, 1955, pink skin became an enormous political issue when, four miles away from our white high school, Rosa Parks refused to give up her seat on the bus.

I had been riding the city bus since I was a small child, so the segregated seating seemed perfectly natural to me. The metal plate above the window in the middle of the bus directed "white" to the front and "colored" to the back. If the white section filled up, and a white woman was standing, we little white gentlemen were taught to surrender our seat to the woman. If there was no more sitting and standing room in the white section, then one of the black passengers was expected to surrender a seat and stand.

I was a senior in the all-white high school, and not one of our teachers dared mention the Bus Boycott, which launched the modern civil rights movement. At home I asked what the fuss was all about, but my older siblings and parents didn't want to discuss it. I persisted, which caused them to call me a "free thinker." I had to think about that. Was that a good thing or bad?

Not Crying at the University of Alabama

OVER THOSE THREE YEARS OF high school my academic performance was not stellar, but I comfortably passed most of my courses. We had no school counselors back then, but I badly needed one. During my senior year I failed typing, which meant I was one-half credit short of having enough credits to graduate. Dorothy called the school to plead my case but was refused. At the end of the school year I sat in the audience and watched my classmates—some since first grade—cross the stage and get their diplomas. I re-took the typing course in summer school and received my diploma in the principal's office in the middle of July.

After leaving summer school I worked a while longer at my bag boy job at the A&P then quit to go to college. My preparation for college was as poor as it had been for entering first grade. By this time Buddy had completed medical school, residency, and two years in the Army. Since his discharge a year before, he was living at home and working at the local VA hospital. There had been no talk of me going to college, and I had never seriously thought about it myself. That changed one day in late August when Buddy announced I was going to the University of Alabama, and he would drive me up there in a couple of weeks.

As I was at Cloverdale School in 1944, in September of 1956 I found myself "abandoned" in Tuscaloosa, Alabama, but I didn't cry that time. I was just disoriented even though I had gone through Orientation, which was required for all freshmen. I really didn't know what a fraternity was, but at the urging of a family friend I quickly found myself "pledged" to one. Having enrolled so late, I had no chance to get into a dormitory, so I found a room in a rooming house close to the campus.

Seven months earlier Arthurine Lucy, a young black woman, had been admitted to the University, but three days later she had been expelled "for her own protection." I occasionally heard the taunts from Auburn students and fans, shouting "Arthurine, Arthurine, Alabama's beauty queen!"

Absent-Minded Harris

A FEW WEEKS AFTER STARTING college I took a weekend trip to Birmingham to visit Margie and George. On Sunday night I demonstrated why I had earned the reputation of being absent-minded. Today some of my family and friends say I have been an absent-minded professor my whole life.

I traveled to Birmingham with my cousin Jerry James, also a student at Alabama, but he would not be returning to campus at the same time I was. Arrangements were made for me to go back by Greyhound bus, which stopped a few blocks from their house.

George drove me to the bus stop, which was in front of Carnaggio's Italian Restaurant on the main road southwest of the city. Since I had a few minutes before the bus arrived, I stepped into the restaurant and ordered a coffee. While I waited there deep in thought, the bus came and went. I was too embarrassed to tell Margie and George that I missed the bus, so I stuck out my thumb to hitchhike. It took a while, but I eventually got a ride with a semi-trailer truck driver who was going through Tuscaloosa. I arrived on campus around midnight. He let me out on the main road and I walked the few blocks to the rooming house where I lived.

College Romance versus Academics

MY ROMANTIC LIFE SINCE MY "cute" days in junior high had been boring, but it livened up that first semester. The fraternity parties put me in touch—so to speak—with some pretty girls who were as clumsy as I was in that basement lit by small red lights. But we never got past a lot of kissing and a little fondling.

At the boarding house, I shared the upstairs with a half-dozen guys, most of whom were upperclassmen. They taught me how to smoke and drink and carouse. One of them, Elliot, was twenty-five years old and had served in the Air Force. He was a good looking, charming guy with black hair and blue eyes whose quick smile charmed the women. He loved to embarrass me when we went out to a restaurant. One day he told the young waitress, with skinny me sitting there, that I was unbelievably well-endowed.

During my teaching life I told my students that my mother thought I was majoring in journalism, but it was really Wine, Women and Song. As a consequence of that "change of major," I finished the fall semester with 2 C's, 2 D's and 2 F's, which put me on academic probation. This of course greatly displeased Buddy, who saw no reason why I should have done so poorly. That ended his financial support, which ended my college education. I returned home for further instructions, which turned out to be that I would go with Buddy when he moved to California to join a friend of his in practice outside San Francisco.

California, There I Went

ONE DAY IN MARCH, 1957, Buddy and I drove out the south end of the semi-circular driveway in front of our house and headed north. I would not have minded if he had then driven in the north end of the driveway, back to where we started. The family and friends waving goodbye would have been surprised and perplexed, but so what? I would have been able to stay home. But he pressed the accelerator and we headed north then west.

We took the southern route across Texas because Buddy's plan was to leave me in San Bernardino, California with Janice and Dan while he got settled in Millbrae, outside San Francisco. We had an uneventful but pleasing drive through the Southwest and discovered how dry and expansive it was. The verdant, irrigated fields of California were a welcome change of scenery.

He dropped me off with Janice and Dan. During the next few weeks I had a lot of time on my hands to consider the trajectory of my life, and I decided that it would be better if I finally took charge instead of being shuffled about. I decided to join the military. The Navy had given James a direction for his life, so why not me? It had given him not only direction but also self-discipline, which served him well while working as an ambulance driver at the college infirmary and finishing his pre-veterinary coursework at Auburn.

Dan was an active duty Air Force major at that time, so he was able to give me good counsel about military life. I called Buddy and told him my decision. He tried to dissuade me and even had other family members call, but I stuck to my decision and enlisted on May 1, 1957.

Silver Treasure APRIL 1957

Buddy's photo of Harris, Dorothy, Dean
[family friend] and Daddy

Boot Camp

BOOT CAMP WAS AND STILL is the most sobering event of my life. The alien conditions of that first day were made more alien before dawn the next morning when we went through the mess line. I was shocked by being served potatoes for breakfast. They might as well have served me broccoli. But I learned to like them, and today I like well-made hash browns more than grits. Our days were filled with classes and constant drilling on the "grinder," a huge parade ground.

The fat boys became slim and muscular; the skinny boys like me gained muscle. My weight got up to about 140. I was so healthy that even though I suffered from anemia as a child and had to be given "liver shots," I was able to donate when they took us to the naval hospital and told us to give blood.

We were constantly told if for whatever reason we couldn't keep up we would have to be put back in another recruit company, which meant more time in boot camp. The Asian flu was sweeping the country, and I got it. I tried to hide that I was sick, but one day while standing in line I fainted and woke up in my bunk. As my flu required only two days of sick leave, I was sent back to my company. All went well for the next few weeks, and it wasn't long before I joined my "shipmates" in developing a "short timers" attitude.

The Day I Got Dressed Up to Get Dressed Down for Being Undressed

It was a warm Friday afternoon, and we "short timers" in our seventh week were cleaning our barracks for the weekly Friday morning captain's inspection.

In keeping with routine, we were washing the decks (floors) and bulkheads (walls) with soap and water (when the Navy says clean they mean clean). It being a warm June day, we being "seasoned" recruits, and (most importantly) most of us being teenagers, we found ourselves in a water fight. Before long there wasn't a member of Company 159 that wasn't drenched in soapy water.

Those of us who were thoroughly soaked took off all of our clothes and continued the fun completely naked. Before long, we discovered how slippery the linoleum floor was and began "skating" on the soapy water. Then one of the guys got a running start, dropped to the floor and slid along on his bare rump. Soon we were having a contest to see who could slide the farthest on his rump. Whoever's turn it was would stand at one end of the barracks and get a running start before hitting the floor and sliding some fifty or sixty feet.

When it was my second or third turn, I was determined to set a new record, so I got a good, fast start, hit the floor at my best speed yet, and was caught up in the exhilaration of the moment. After a few seconds I noticed that the barracks had suddenly gone completely quiet. All the other recruits were standing at attention at the foot of their bunks, some fully clothed, and some partially clothed, some naked, but all dripping soapy water.

Then I looked down at the other end of the barracks and saw, to my horror, the Company Commander standing in the hatch (doorway). I tried desperately to stop but couldn't. My soapy hands could not get traction on the soapy floor. Powerless to stop, I slid right up to his feet and jumped to attention. When all was utterly quiet, with eighty young men standing rigidly at attention, the Commander spoke. "YOU CLOWNS GET IN THOSE DRESS UNIFORMS AND BE IN FRONT OF BATTALION HQ IN FIVE MINUTES!"

Never before or since have I dressed so fast. Forget drying off. We snatched our skivvies and dress uniforms out of our lockers and furiously threw on our pants and jumper, dress shoes, and white hats. We jerked the rolled kerchief under the collar flap and frantically tied the square knot in front while running to fall in. In slightly less than five minutes all eighty of us were in uniform, at attention, on the parade ground in front of HQ. We were looking pretty sharp despite an occasional fleck of soap suds in someone's hair or on someone's navy blue sleeve.

After a minute or two the Company Commander and the battalion CO strolled out of the building and stood in front of us. For what seemed a very long time, they just stood there, and the silence was penetrating.

Off in some distant barracks a radio was playing. I could barely hear the music. It was the young crooner Pat Boone: "Yew made a vow . . . that yew . . . would always be trew . . . but somehow . . . that vow . . . meant nothing to yew . . . ."

When the Company Commander finally spoke, he blistered our ears. Then he had me and two others report "FRONT AND CENTER!" for additional remarks. Following that, he told us to "FALL OUT!"

Becoming a Navy Hospital Corpsman

FOLLOWING BOOT CAMP, I WAS assigned to the U.S. Naval Hospital where we had given blood. I entered the Hospital Corps School compound on the grounds of the hospital, where I was trained to be a corpsman (a "medic"). Upon graduation four months later I was assigned to ward duty at that hospital. My patients were both active duty military and veterans.

My first assignment was to ENT, where we treated everything from tonsillectomies to terminal throat cancer. During the four months I was assigned there on a "port-starboard" schedule (24 hours on, 24 off), I provided nursing care for two men in their fifties. One was a Navy veteran in the last stages of throat cancer. He cautiously walked around the ward barely able to hold up his head due to weakened neck muscles. He had a permanent tracheotomy we kept clean, and we gave him enough morphine to keep him almost free of pain. The nurses supervised the dispensing of narcotics. He died without much suffering along the way.

The second ENT patient was a heavy smoker I met when my schedule was changed to night duty, which meant working from 7:00 p.m. to 7:00 a.m. every day for one month. He was bald and looked nice and healthy when first admitted, but he told me he had cancer of the jaw and his main chance for survival required that his lower jaw be removed, which he refused. When he asked me to buy him a carton of cigarettes at the hospital "ship's store," I saw nothing wrong with his request and brought the cigarettes the next night.

Over the next couple of weeks I provided his nighttime nursing care and talked to him about life. His face, then his whole head, began to swell so badly that his facial features were horribly distorted, so we put free-standing curtains around his bed to keep him from scaring other patients and their visitors. Toward the end he became disoriented. One day while visitors were present, he stumbled out from behind his curtains, and a few of the visitors close by jumped up and ran a few feet away.

Another memory I have of those months in ENT was of the night nurse who patrolled the wards, checking on the corpsmen. We sat in the nurse's station discussing politics. She was from Massachusetts and was very impressed by the presidential prospects of the handsome young senator from her state, John F. Kennedy.

Sometimes It's Good to be Late

AMONG THE MANY DUTIES I had was working emergency room shifts. One Friday morning when I arrived for duty a little late I learned that sometimes it's good to be late. When I arrived, all of the corpsmen, nurses and doctors were preparing for captain's inspection. They were busy performing one kind of cleaning or organizing duty or other.

The scene was a kaleidoscope of white and khaki uniforms, white smocks and gleaming, stainless steel surfaces. Oil of wintergreen enlivened the nose. I decided I'd better check the patients in case any had not been checked recently. As I walked between the beds in the ER ward I saw a large notice hanging from the foot of a bed. It read "BP q 15 min." With everybody so busy I decided the blood pressure reading could easily be overdue. I stopped by the man's bed to talk to him and take his BP.

He looked to be in his forties. He had blond hair and a boyishness face, but his eyes looked much older. I wondered what he must have seen during WWII. I saw that his diagnosis was bleeding ulcer. We chatted pleasantly while I arranged the cuff and stethoscope. When I was ready, I studied the gauge while pumping up the cuff. When I released the pressure the needle dropped all the way to zero. At first I thought something was wrong with the cuff, but when I glanced up at the patient his eyes had rolled back in his head. Then blood gushed from both ends of his body. I yelled and everyone came running.

The surgeon on duty took a scalpel and cut into both ankles to find blood vessels his surgical team could use to infuse whole blood directly into his body using large needles and syringes. The scene was controlled chaos. In just a few minutes they had infused enough blood to be able to wheel him into the operating room. We were so busy for the rest of the day I didn't get a chance to check on him. Turns out I never heard if he survived or not. I like to think that he did survive and that I saved his life.

Practicing my Spanish in a Tijuana Strip Club

LIKE MOST OF MY FELLOW sailors, one of the reasons I joined the Navy was to see the world. I wanted to broaden myself, so I would occasionally visit the "broads" in the bars of Tijuana, Mexico, ten miles south. Our main destination was the Navy Club. There the girls greeted us warmly and invited us to sit at tables surrounding the dance floor.

In return for their company we were obliged to buy the girls drinks. Still underage at that time I ordered nothing for myself even though I probably could have in Mexico. The drinks of clear liquid in shot glasses were probably water, but we gladly paid, every few minutes, one dollar a drink, for the attention of the girls.

On one occasion I decided to impress my girl with the Spanish I had studied for two years at Lanier High. My conversational Spanish was limited, and I used what I could. I decided to impress my girl by reciting something I had been required to memorize in Spanish II: "The Lord's Prayer." I don't recall how I was able to work it into the conversation, but I got it said: "*Padre nuestro que estas in los cielos, santificado sea tu nombre . . . .*" After I said *Amen,* the girl was speechless and just sat there. I got the distinct impression that I was the first Anglo-American sailor to recite to her the Lord's Prayer in Spanish. She lost interest in having me buy her "drinks," and not long after that my buddies and I found ourselves in a taxicab headed back to San Diego.

Frank's Final Fling

ONE DAY IN APRIL, 1958, while assigned to the urology ward, I arrived for duty and discovered that a fellow corpsman, David Holden, and I had been assigned to the care of an 84-year-old veteran of the Spanish-American War, whom we came to know as Frank. He had been sent to our ward for treatment of a bladder disorder.

His main problem was advanced syphilis. His spinal cord and brain were so diseased that he couldn't walk, and he was completely disoriented. He had been bedridden for years, which caused very bad decubitus ulcers (bed sores). Our most unpleasant duty was to treat those ulcers. David was a muscular young cowboy from Wyoming with a winning personality. He was always laughing about one thing or another. Therefore, I could not have had a better workmate for such a distasteful job.

Since Frank was disconnected from reality and felt no pain, he seemed to be quite contented all the time. If he wasn't sleeping peacefully, he was looking around and mumbling. He had been a career sergeant in the Army, so when his mumbles were more animated than usual David and I liked to think he was giving orders to his troops. He didn't know who we were and had no interest in what we were doing.

Yes, the job of cleaning and caring for him each day was unpleasant, but what bothered us more was the wall between him and us. We wanted to reach him, to get him to respond to us. He was always lying on his back, and one day while standing at the foot of his bed, David reached out and pulled his toe. Even though Frank had no feeling below his waist, the movement of his upper body from the pull got his attention. His bushy, white eyebrows knitted and his brow furrowed. His black eyes lit up, and his jowls quivered. His mouth opened slightly, and he croaked, "Stop that!"

It was almost like he had awakened from the dead. David and I were pleased to have a cranky old man to care for. After that, we pulled his toe to get his attention when we arrived. We talked to him during his bath and treatments. We joked with him and kidded him. He was just Frank, one of the guys, even though he could have been our great grandfather. He mumbled very little, but his eyes followed our movements, and they seemed to shine at times.

Treating him like a pal made our daily routines more tolerable. After flushing out his in-dwelling catheter and emptying his urine bag, we bathed him from head to foot and combed his thick, white hair to make him as presentable as we could for the nurses, doctors and other corpsmen, for Frank never got any visitors. Next we cleaned and medicated his ulcers and tried to find ways to relieve the pressure that cut off the blood circulation, which caused the ulceration. The pressure on his tailbone had made the entire sacral region necrotic. The ulcer was the size of a man's hand and about an inch deep.

Since he felt no pain, he would sleep through our ministrations. Occasionally he would wake up and ask us what we were doing, as in "Hey! Whatcha doin' there!?" To him, we were a couple of guys who came to his room from time to time and bothered him. So he would tell us to get out of his room. One day when he said that David crawled in bed next to him and Frank started yelling for the police. I stepped out into the hallway and got a Marine I saw passing by. Dressed in his green uniform and billed garrison cap, the Marine looked a lot like a policeman, so I had him come in and "arrest" David, with great fanfare. That may have been the only time we ever saw Frank smile. Getting David "arrested" must have pleased him very much.

We grew quite fond of the old man. We spent as much time as we could with him. We teased him a lot because we believed that the stimulation was good for his blood circulation. A couple of times we put him in a wheelchair and took him all over the wards to visit the other patients and the staff. He seemed to enjoy the attention they gave him. He had been prescribed a soft diet, but one day we decided he would enjoy a regular diet, so we pulled one off the cart, put it in front of him, and told him to eat it. He ate the whole thing. From then on he got a regular diet, and one day we saw him put away two complete dinners.

He looked like he was gaining weight, and his color was better, so we started weighing him every day. By the third week his ulcers had improved a little bit, and he had gained ten pounds. Even though it was hard to tell what Frank was thinking, David and I decided that he liked us. This made us feel good because as far as we knew we were the only friends he had. We also decided that as a career soldier he had never married and just made a life for himself in the Army.

After about a month of daily contact with Frank, we came to work one day and found him gone. We checked at the nursing station and learned that his bladder treatment was finished so he had been transferred to General Medicine on the other side of the hospital grounds. David and I went over to see him and found that he had been put on a Stryker frame. Designed for spinal injuries, the frame attached to the head and feet and kept the patient suspended in air. In this way his ulcers should get better because his skin would get no pressure. We noticed his meal was sitting on his bedside table, uneaten.

I never went back to see him, but David went every day and loudly complained about nobody feeding Frank, nobody teasing him. I was sure he exaggerated about the feeding. It just wasn't done his way. I was surprised he didn't get in trouble. In less than a week Frank was dead. David and I felt like we had lost a close friend. Not long afterward he and I were given assignments in different areas of the hospital and lost touch with each other.

At first we saw Frank's care only as an unpleasant duty we were ordered to perform. But in just a few days we no longer saw a nasty, semi-comatose old man and began to see a great-grandfather we wished we had met sooner. I treasure having been a part of Frank's Final Fling.

Nurses and Corpsmen

AN INTERESTING DYNAMIC OF WARD duty was the interaction between the corpsmen (enlisted men) and nurses (officers). We were supervised by these nurses and worked closely with them on shift, but we were not of course allowed to "fraternize" with them, even though we were about the same age as many of them.

On one assignment I found myself being supervised by Miss Throyer, who was more like a Marine D.I. than a nurse. Behind her back we called her "Misstroyer." It became apparent to us that she was so strict because she was so young and so new to the military. All of us had been in the Navy for a while and could be a little intimidating. The most intimidating was Brown, who was the old man at about twenty-five. He had spent time on board ship before going to hospital corps school.

Because of her stern deportment, I considered Miss Throyer quite ugly. Her five-foot frame had absolutely no figure. Her red hair looked like red steel wool—and probably felt like it, too. Her pasty white skin was covered with disgusting rust-colored freckles. Over time, however, an amazing thing happened. As she gained more self-confidence and became more relaxed, she underwent a transformation. Her hair softened and developed a little wave. She actually knew how to smile, and her smile was pretty. Her skin developed a pleasing pink hue, and her freckles became cute. Most amazing of all for us young men: she developed a figure.

One day I learned that she and Brown were getting married. I was shocked by the violation of Navy regulations and hoped they would not get into trouble. Then I thought about the match and realized it was good. He was a few years older than she and only a few inches taller. And after the real Miss Throyer emerged, I realized they had similar, light-hearted personalities. The wedding party at the justice of the peace included just the couple and a handful of corpsmen.

Another of our nurse supervisors on that ward was Miss Fox, who looked a little older than Miss Throyer and much more self-confident. Of normal height with a very nice figure and a pretty face, Miss Fox made a strong impression on us corpsmen. I actually had a crush on her and longed to press her ample curves against my skinny frame. One of my best buddies on the ward was Winkler, a big, good looking country boy from Arkansas. We shared our fantasies about Miss Fox.

One day he told me that he and Miss Fox were getting married and asked if I would be his best man. I don't know if the invitation to be best man was to soothe my broken heart or to inflict further damage, but I agreed and joined another small group at the office of the justice of the peace downtown.

Following the weddings I never saw either couple again. From time to time I think about Mr. and Mrs. Brown and Mr. and Mrs. Winkler. Did the marriages last? Did they stay in the Navy? I hope both couples are still together, old and gray but happy.

On Leave and Alabama Bound

DURING MY TIME IN SAN Diego, I took a few trips to Alabama to refresh my soul. The first two were by bus, on either Greyhound or Trailways. Although I did miss my family and was certainly refreshed when seeing them again, I was more refreshed by seeing and smelling the vegetation of the Southeast.

The natural beauty of southern California was somehow not natural because of the heavy dependence on irrigation to turn the brown terrain green. On open highways outside of the city, the hillsides were brown and dry. The ubiquitous eucalyptus trees were dry and dusty. I suppose I found the ambience so arid because "home" for me required lots of moisture, including humidity. The first trip was just after leaving boot camp and I was conscious of nothing but getting home. On the second trip a year later I spent many hours looking out the window at sand or dirt, cacti, mesquite and tumbleweeds, a scene which is beautiful in its own way, but still not "home."

When we reached east Texas, my heart quickened when I realized the trees were getting taller and greener and more plentiful. By the time we reached Louisiana and made a stop, I stepped off the bus and deeply inhaled the thick air redolent of honeysuckle and magnolia and jasmine. I actually enjoyed the humidity and sweating. As the bus continued on toward Mississippi, I saw a tree house behind a farmhouse and a tire swing in front. I could not remember seeing a tree house out West, let alone a tire swing.

In May of 1959, I took a two-week leave with my friend and fellow corpsman Ken Zane, a very likeable, carefree California con artist with a lust for life. Our trip, I realize now, was something like those Jack Kerouac describes in *On the Road,* but Ken was a much saner version of Kerouac's Dean. I was head corpsman for the hospital Officer of the Day's office, and Ken was one of my men. A few months earlier, while on a month-long night shift, he worked at a private hospital during the day to make extra money for his upcoming discharge. He asked me if I minded him napping in the ambulance between runs since he was tired from getting no sleep during the daytime. I was happy to oblige until I found out he was telling his private hospital supervisor about working all night at the naval hospital. Apparently he got more sleep than any of us.

In preparation for our cross-country run, we got some casual-wear civvies and a very close haircut. I don't exactly recall what kind of image we were cultivating, but we planned to have a good time. Janice and Dan had helped me buy a white, 1953 Mercury, and after getting my car serviced and gassed up, we loaded up our shaving kits, a few changes of clothes in a bag of some sort, and our bongo drums. I use the term "my car" very loosely because Ken talked me into giving him a key, and he drove it at least as much as I did.

At a time when there were no interstate highways, we set out on U.S. 80 for Montgomery, Alabama, 2300 miles away, at a maximum legal speed limit of sixty miles per hour. One of us drove while the other either slept or played the bongo drums in the back seat. On a few occasions while driving, Ken slammed on the brakes in the middle of a long, desolate stretch and ran around to the front of the car where he jumped up and shouted "Yaa-hoo!" a few times. No, we were not drinking alcohol or smoking dope. Except for Ken's spontaneous demonstrations we stopped only to get gas and some kind of food, and to use a bathroom, if necessary.

We arrived forty-seven hours after leaving our barracks at the hospital, at an average speed of about fifty. We were warmly welcomed by Dorothy and John, who lived on a farm south of the city. I spent the next week or so showing my California friend Alabama and Florida, and he had a wonderful time. He even got to drive John's tractor. I don't remember much about our return trip, so it must have been much more conventional. Not long after we got back, Ken was discharged from the Navy and I lost touch with him—but *not* with my car.

While on my Way to the Fleet Marine Force (FMF)

A YEAR OR SO LATER, even though I had requested a transfer to the east coast, I was sent west to Hawaii. In the fall of 1959 I was assigned to the Fleet Marine Force and transferred to the Marine infantry training facility at Del Mar, California. Following one month of training, I took a short leave of absence to spend time with Buddy in San Francisco, where I would depart for Hawaii from Treasure Island naval base.

Richard was also a hospital corpsman, and he was stationed at the naval hospital in Oakland, across the bay from San Francisco. James was now enrolled in veterinary medicine at Auburn and was spending the summer with Buddy while working at a local box factory to make money for college. For a week or so we enjoyed the city, which included rubbing elbows with beatniks in the North Beach section. Among the night spots we visited were the Purple Onion, the Hungry i, and a not so "beat" place called Two Beers and Everybody Sings. At one of the spots where showing ID was enforced, we made advance preparations. James, twenty-six, gave me his ID, and I, twenty-one, gave mine to Richard, barely nineteen. The scheme worked.

One day James and I went grocery shopping for the apartment. On our way back, just a block from home, James failed to notice a stop sign and a car hit the door on my side. The impact caused the car to veer left and crash through a hedge into a neighbor's yard. Nobody was seriously hurt, but my door was badly damaged. James exchanged information with the other driver then drove the short distance to the apartment while I held the door closed. While we were negotiating with the people in the other car, Buddy drove home. He got out of his car and peered up the street at us. Exasperated, he shook his head and walked into the building.

Since we had dates that night, we tied the passenger door closed and just used the driver's side door. We hurriedly showered and got dressed.

I had a small laceration on my scalp where my head had shattered the side window, but after I stopped the bleeding and dabbed a little iodine on the wound, I was ready to go. Our dates didn't seem to mind getting in and out on the driver's side or riding in our rolling wreck.

A few days later my leave ended and I reported to my ship. On board were eight hundred soldiers, all of them just out of boot camp. I estimate 799 of them got seasick. I quickly learned not to stand next to the ship's railing when a soldier was standing at the railing upwind. I just missed getting hit by a full-load upchuck.

One day when it was okay to be topside, I noticed military dependents on the upper decks of the ship, an area off-limits to us. I was impressed by how much nicer their accommodations were than our "racks" in the hold of the ship. I promised myself that one day I would travel on a luxury ocean liner. Almost fifty years later, my wife and I took a cruise, but the difference was not as great as I thought it would be—but of course I was no longer twenty-one.

Aloha ha

IN NOVEMBER, 1959, HAWAII WAS our brand new 50th state. We thought we would get a warm welcome—alohas, leis, wiggling grass skirts. Nope. When we docked at Pearl Harbor, we were unceremoniously loaded into trucks for a ride over the Pali Mountains to Kaneohe Bay, home of the First Marine Brigade. During our first week on base the Kilauea volcano erupted on the big island of Hawaii, which added to the excitement statehood had brought. Airplane trips to view the eruption were available for tourists

A few months later, in May of 1960, a tsunami left Chile headed for Hawaii. That event brought more excitement than the citizens of the new state wanted. All troops at Kaneohe were ordered to shoulder infantry backpacks and go to two-story buildings on base. There we sat in the second story hallways and leaned against the walls. The tsunami just missed Oahu and slammed into the harbor city of Hilo on the big island. Sixty-one people were killed and 540 homes and businesses were destroyed.

Life as a Grunt

As THE COMPANY CORPSMAN OF Golf Company, Second Battalion, Fourth Regiment, First Marine Brigade, my three platoon corpsmen and I were sent out on training exercises, mostly to the island of Molokai, famous for its pineapple fields and its leper colony. I never had contact with any lepers, but I do remember sleeping on the ground in a pineapple field. I had no tent and used my first aid kit as a pillow.

In February of 1960 the Brigade boarded a troop ship at Pearl Harbor and sailed to Taiwan to play war games with the Third Marine Division, stationed on Okinawa. Before the ship got underway, I was so busy getting my troops taken care of that I did not lay claim to one of the bunks (which were five deep from overhead to deck). I spent the first night on the steel deck of the compartment. We all slept with our infantry backpacks. I wedged myself into the horseshoe shape in order not to roll around on the deck when the ship put out to sea.

Our joint assignment was to dissuade Mao Tse Tung from invading Taiwan. Mao had shelled the Taiwanese islands of Quemoy and Matsu and was sounding more and more bellicose. After a few weeks of war games with the Third Division and the Seventh Fleet, which patrolled the Formosa Straits, Mao responded to our "saber rattling" and backed down.

During our lengthy bivouac in the jungles of southern Taiwan, a number of pimps and prostitutes operated just outside the camp perimeter. We corpsmen could do nothing to control the operation and just hoped that the troops remembered what we had taught them about avoiding V.D. Many didn't listen or didn't care. After we left Kaohsiung for four days of R&R in Yokosuka, Japan, I was instructed to give the troops a "short-arm" inspection.

Early one morning when we were about halfway to Japan, my three corpsmen and I stood at the foot of the "ladders" from our compartment to the five "heads" on the next deck up. Each troop had to show his penis then "milk" it as one would a cow teat. We were to note if any pus was excreted and take the name of any man who was infected. We had

71

to do this before the man urinated, which would wash out any pus in his urethra. Speaking of the heads, if for some reason someone didn't get to a head before it closed at about 0730, he was not allowed to use it because it was being cleaned. I don't know what the troops did, but we corpsmen could relieve ourselves in the ship's sickbay.

As you can imagine, discipline was very strict. Even though our sixteen-day trip from Hawaii took us across the tropical waters of the south Pacific, we were not allowed to undo the top button of our heavy fatigue uniforms except in our sleeping quarters. We were also not allowed to "uncover." A "shave tail" second lieutenant chewed me out one day for having my fatigue cap pushed back from my eyebrows.

We had a wonderful time in Japan. In 1960, the dollar was worth 350 yen, so being a tourist was inexpensive. A night out on the town in Yokosuka could cost only a few dollars. Unfortunately, some of the troops had a better time than they should have.

On our way back to Hawaii, we Marine corpsmen helped the ship's corpsmen treat 113 cases of gonorrhea and other venereal diseases. The troops had "made contact" with the prostitutes of Taiwan or Japan or both. When we sailed back into Pearl Harbor, I saw some of our married patients squirm as they waved to their wives on the pier, wives they hadn't seen for a couple of months.

Infantry to Infirmary

EVEN THOUGH I ENJOYED SERVING in the infantry, a few weeks after we returned to base I asked to be transferred from Golf Company to the base infirmary. I wanted to take night classes at the University of Hawaii, and that wouldn't work if I had to be ready at all times for a training exercise on another island. My transfer was approved, and for the rest of my military service I was assigned to the infirmary.

I eventually completed advanced college degrees, but that ten-month period at the infirmary was the most educational ten months of my life. Not long after I arrived, the corpsman in charge left, and I took his place. There were four of us working under the supervision of a civilian registered nurse who oversaw our unit and the infirmary ward. But she had enough confidence in us that she rarely came by.

Our unit included the Emergency Room and the Central Supply Room where all supplies and equipment were procured and maintained. Back in those days before disposable medical waste we sterilized medical equipment like syringes in an autoclave. The hypodermic needles were also re-usable, but we had to use sandstone to sharpen their bevels before they were sterilized.

Next to the CSR was the minor surgery room. Across the hall from minor surgery was the emergency delivery room where dependent wives could deliver their babies if they didn't have enough time to make it across the mountains to Tripler Army Hospital. Next to that room was the cast room where we helped apply plaster casts to broken limbs.

The Navy doctors also gave us a high degree of autonomy. One of them told me that if a Marine came to the ER with a scalp wound, which could have resulted from something like a bar fight on Hotel Street in Honolulu, then put my finger in the hole. If the skull feels normally curved, sew him up. If there is a depression in the skull, contact the doctor on call to come have a look.

Military Circumcisions

ONE OF OUR DOCTORS WAS Jewish, and one day when I accompanied him on sick call, my clipboard in hand, he asked each Marine if he had been circumcised. If not he had me schedule him for surgery. He also told me to get a certain kind of scissors for the operations. I assisted him as he wielded his special, curved scissors.

In the urology ward at the Naval Hospital in San Diego, in addition to severe cases like Frank we had healthy young men who were circumcised for a variety of reasons. Because circumcision involves removing skin from around the head of the penis, the surgeon had to close the wound with several sturdy sutures. These young men would sometime get erections, which not only hurt horribly but could even pop the stitches.

We kept several ampules of amyl nitrate on the patient's bedside table in case of an erection. He could just break the ampule and sniff the drug, which would immediately cause the penis to collapse. One of our less intelligent patients was thumbing through something like *Playboy* when he started howling. I saw him fumbling with everything on his table as he tried to find an ampule. The middle-aged nurse on duty briskly marched over to his bed, jerked his sheet back, whipped her ball point pen out of her dress pocket, and whacked the head of his engorged penis, which immediately wilted.

Babies on Board

IN THE EMERGENCY DELIVERY ROOM at the infirmary, we kept a sterilized OB kit containing everything needed to perform a normal delivery. Just inside the doorway on a stainless steel table we kept sterile rubber gloves. Over those ten months I assisted with four deliveries and learned about such matters as episiotomies.

The most memorable of these deliveries occurred when we got a woman who was about to deliver any second. One of the guys notified the doctors to come STAT while the rest of us were lifting her up on the delivery table. While she was still suspended over the table, the baby's head appeared, so I very reluctantly placed my hands under the baby, ready to catch it. Just before it fell out, one of the doctors burst into the room, snatched on the gloves and caught the baby as it fell.

Pulchritude and Philosophy

As for those college classes, I enrolled in English composition the same month I started at the infirmary. I had failed the course at the University of Alabama, so I decided to pretend I had never taken the class and would start fresh. The dean somehow learned of my academic probation at Alabama and said that I was on probation at Hawaii, which meant I had to perform or be expelled. We Marines and corpsmen taking night classes at the university gathered at a central point to board a bus which took us over the mountains to the campus in Honolulu.

My English 101 class had about a dozen students, mostly male, and was taught by the most beautiful teacher I've ever had. Mrs. Jones was twenty-four, shapely, and intoxicating. She had thick red hair and green eyes. On temporary assignment to the University of Hawaii from the University of California, Berkley, she was Israeli and had recently completed her required military service in Israel.

She wore bright, multi-colored sarongs to class, sometimes complemented by an orchid in her hair. She sat on the edge of her desk, crossed her legs and lectured on the likes of Frederick Nietzsche and Simone de Beauvoir while smoking a cigarette and bouncing a sandal on her dainty toe. When she had us write in class, she would stroll up and down the aisles, pausing to look over a student's shoulder to see how the writing progressed. When she paused at my desk and put her head down next to mine, her perfume made me drunk with desire, and I had no idea what I was writing or what she was saying.

She was evasive about her husband, so we never learned anything about that lucky, lucky man. The idea that he might enjoy being separated from her was inconceivable to us men. At the end of the term she invited the whole class to a beer party at her grass shack on the campus, which served as temporary faculty housing. Only the men showed up. After being served Filipino beer, we were instructed to sit in a circle on the floor on pillows. She sat in the middle of the circle on several pillows. During our conversation with her, we learned that she was returning to California and needed to sell her green 1949

Ford convertible. I bought it for $90 but was never able to get it safety certified by base security, so I had to park it outside the main gate. My buddies and I enjoyed many trips around Oahu and for a while even rented an apartment in Honolulu so we could pretend to be civilians.

When Barack Obama was running for president, I learned that his parents had been at the University of Hawaii at the same time I was, but they were in day classes. If in 1960 somebody had told me that a black man from Kenya and a white woman from Kansas would have a baby boy who would become president of the United States, I could not have believed it.

Hold High Your Head, Tom Dooley

A FEW MONTHS BEFORE MY discharge from the Navy, I heard about a Dr. Tom Dooley, a civilian who was in Honolulu looking for medics being discharged. He wanted them to join his expedition to some place called Vietnam. He wanted to set up medical facilities in the jungle for those being injured in skirmishes among warring factions.

One of my fellow corpsmen at the infirmary, Dave Curbow, was also getting discharged, so he and I considered staying in Hawaii and joining Dr. Dooley's mission. The whole idea sounded romantic and swashbuckling. We could see ourselves working alongside the heroic doctor, helping to save the lives of those primitive people. I could see my picture in *Life* magazine handing Dr. Dooley an abdominal bandage, both of us in sweat-soaked fatigues leaning over a half-naked fighter covered in blood.

Dave and I decided that, as appealing as that sounded, we needed to continue working on our college degrees. Long after I finished my degrees and was completing my teaching career, I learned that if Dave and I had gone with Dr. Dooley he might have tried to make the experience more romantic than swashbuckling. According to my source, he was especially interested in male medics in their early twenties.

Now that I have Google, I researched Tom Dooley and learned that he had been a corpsman like us but had gone to medical school after discharge and re-entered the Navy as a doctor. He was later accused of homosexual behavior and discharged from service. His devotion to serving the medical needs of the poor of Southeast Asia is quite true, and he distinguished himself very admirably until his death from melanoma at age thirty-four. I learned that John F. Kennedy cited the example of Dr. Dooley when he launched the Peace Corps.

Now that I know the full story of Dr. Dooley, I'm sorry I didn't take my chance to work with him. A man as noble as he was could not have been a sexual predator. He would have been more like an older man I served with. I suspected he was homosexual, but he treated me like a younger brother.

Civilian Life and a Trip Home

IN APRIL, 1961 I WAS discharged from the Navy at Treasure Island. I decided to stay in the Bay area for a while, so I moved in with Buddy. Shortly after getting settled in his apartment, I took a trip back to Montgomery to see my family. Dave Curbow went with me.

We traveled down to San Bernardino where Janice and Dan lent us their second car, a 1960 Mercury Comet. Since Dave didn't drive, I had to do all the driving. We spent the first night in El Paso, which is on the far western tip of Texas. The next morning we were ready to go by seven o'clock. I was feeling especially good, so I told Dave we would be smelling that fragrant Louisiana air before bedtime.

On the long flat stretches, I sometimes hit eighty. On one occasion, we entered a cut in a hill at about eighty. The cut provided a windbreak, but when we topped the hill we went airborne and flew past the protection of the cut. A strong gust of wind slammed into the car, and we landed on the shoulder on the other side of the road, skidding sideways. Lucky for us the car didn't roll over.

When I think back to the '59 trip, Ken and I didn't go airborne like that because the old Mercury was much heavier than the Comet, which was so basic it didn't even have a heater. As with the earlier auto trip, we stopped only for gas, snack food and necessary head calls. At 7:00 p.m. we reached Marshall, Texas, where we made a pit stop. When I got out of the car my legs were shaking so much I had trouble walking. I gave up and we took a room in another cheap motel, about one hundred miles short of Louisiana.

A Tale of Two Buses

IN 1961, WHEN AN INTER-STATE bus crossed into a southern state, the bus stopped and the black passengers moved to the back. While Dave and I were crossing the country, the Freedom Riders were challenging that segregation law by not moving from their seats. In Anniston, Alabama a mob stopped a Greyhound bus and beat the passengers as they got off. Then they burned the bus.

This occurred just before we reached Montgomery. Some of my family and friends were members of the White Citizens Council, and a few of the men were also something like "deputy sheriffs," which I took to be quasi-official vigilantes. A couple of the "deputies" told me that Martin Luther King, Jr. was scheduled to arrive at the airport with an entourage, and they wanted me to take a shotgun and go with a group of them to the airport to form a "welcoming committee." We were to stand off to the side while holding our shotguns at port arms, across our chests. I declined the offer.

When the replacement bus from Anniston arrived in Montgomery, I was at the bus station to see what would happen. The bus passengers I saw leaving the bus were not bothered. The trouble must have started with the arrival of another bus a few days later after Dave and I had left to go back to California. Historical accounts report that the Alabama National Guard had to be brought in to quell the violence. Today the old Greyhound station in Montgomery is a Freedom Riders museum.

Three blocks away is the Rosa Parks museum, which is located in the building next to the city bus stop where she was arrested on December 1, 1955. The bus she was riding at the time has been restored and serves as a "bus museum" in Detroit, where Parks lived from 1957 until her death in 2005.

Letter to the Editor

Editor, *Montgomery Advertiser*
Montgomery, Alabama
November 13, 2007

Dear Editor:

I recently read in the *Atlanta Journal Constitution* about a legislative move in Montgomery to remove the criminal records of those arrested for violating segregation laws. The premier case cited is that of Rosa Parks. Having been a senior at Lanier High School in Montgomery when Ms. Parks was arrested, I have a keen interest in this matter.

I see this move by the legislators as just another gimmick to win votes. Aside from the political gimmickry of the proposal, it is a bad idea because it would remove from the official record what happened during those times, and future generations may have no knowledge of the civil rights struggle. Instead of regarding the arrest records as a stain on the character of Rosa Parks, Martin Luther King, Jr. and the rest, they should be regarded as badges of honor.

Harris Green
Big Canoe, Georgia

Back to California
for College and Employment

SOON AFTER RETURNING TO CALIFORNIA, I enrolled in a sociology class at San Francisco State. Mark Twain once remarked that the coldest winter he ever spent was a summer in San Francisco. I totally agree. I wore an overcoat to class. A black woman was also enrolled. She was my first black classmate.

After finishing that class I transferred to a junior college in San Mateo, a small city south of San Francisco where I had recently obtained a job as an orderly on the men's ward at Mills Memorial Hospital. I took classes in the morning and worked the 3-11 shift at the hospital. Richard completed his enlistment in September of that year and got a job in that hospital as a janitor.

Buddy had recently moved back to Alabama, and Richard and I had taken over his apartment. One of my fellow orderlies was Hawaiian, and one day he asked me if I would like to meet a beautiful blonde. Without hesitating or stuttering, I said yes. She ate supper in the hospital cafeteria each night, just as we did. When he introduced me to her, I immediately decided that "beautiful" was inadequate.

A Viking Invasion of My Heart

HER NAME WAS ANNELISE MADSEN, and she had arrived a couple of weeks before from Copenhagen, Denmark on an immigrant's visa. She was working as a laboratory technologist at the hospital, and as a resident of the Nurses Home across the street Annelise took her meals in the cafeteria. Although she had completed five years of English in Denmark, she had never visited an English speaking country, so she was heavily dependent on her little red Danish-English dictionary.

A year earlier she had been working at a hospital in Copenhagen as a newly graduated lab technologist. One of her workmates had just returned from the United States where she had worked at Mills hospital until her visa expired and she returned to Denmark. Annelise was impressed with her friend's account of life in America, making her want to spend a couple of years living there. The workmate advised her to apply for immigrant status to avoid the time restriction of a visa. In the early sixties, preference was given to immigrant applications from northern Europe.

A year later, immigration papers in hand, together with employment papers from Mills hospital, she flew across the Arctic Circle to San Francisco, via Los Angeles. You could say that all this information gave me an impressive "anatomy" lesson. In addition to her blonde hair, green eyes and huggable body, I was also impressed by her beautiful brains and guts. We had our first date on Halloween night, 1961, and I took her for a night on the town in San Francisco in Richard's 1951 Studebaker. Over the next few months we fell in love.

Annelise's Introduction to American TV

ONE DAY SOON AFTER SHE arrived in the United States, Annelise was watching television in the living room of the Nurses Home by herself. She was engrossed in a drama when it suddenly ended and another program started. She thought that very strange but realized anew how much she had to learn about life in America.

She walked into the kitchen to make herself a sandwich to take upstairs to her room. When she passed back through the living room the drama she had been watching was back on, so she sat down to watch some more of it. Then when the drama suddenly ended again she stayed seated to see what this interruption was all about and learned how American television commercials work.

Lout of the Ring

ONE DAY IN FEBRUARY OF 1962, I was circling the parking lot of a small shopping center while listening to a live broadcast of John Glenn circling the earth. He was describing our planet in glowing terms. Being in love, I too was in orbit, and the earth looked wonderful to me also. I was shopping for an engagement ring for Annelise. I found a small jewelry store, and the owner accepted a down payment on a modest engagement/wedding ring set which cost me a month's salary—$300.

The next day we were in the living room of my apartment, and I got down on one knee to propose. It being George Washington's birthday, I could not tell a lie, so I was under extra pressure to convey the sincerity of my love. It went well until I started to place the ring on her finger and realized I didn't know which hand to take. I asked her, but she didn't know the American custom.

I interrupted the proposal and went into the kitchen to find the San Francisco phone book. I opened it to some place in the middle and stuck my finger next to a number. I called the number, a woman answered, I asked the question, and she told me which hand to take. I then went back into the living room and finished the proposal. Despite my crude effort to be gallant, she agreed to marry me.

Engagement photo of Annelise and Harris

Alabama, Here We Come

WE DECIDED TO MOVE TO Alabama in June and be married there. Janice and Dan agreed to sell us the Comet, so we flew down to San Bernardino. The trip was also a chance for Annelise to meet them. Following a delightful couple of days, we drove back to San Mateo along the coast. When I saw the sign for the famous Hearst Castle in San Simeon, I asked Annelise if she would like to stop. She said no. She had seen enough castles in Denmark. I had never seen a castle, but I didn't tell her that.

I planned to enter Auburn University after we were married, so I applied for admission. I received a letter refusing my request because Auburn still considered me to be on academic probation from Alabama even though by this time I had a B average over a half dozen courses from three colleges. I wrote back, stressing the fact that I was now five years older and had demonstrated my commitment to higher education, which could be shown in my transcripts. They accepted me on probation, and for my first term at Auburn I made the dean's list.

That June we quit our jobs and packed our car with all our worldly possessions. Richard also quit his job at the hospital so he could travel home with us and be the best man at our wedding. In order to carry all our stuff, we had to buy a large wire basket which we strapped to the roof of the car. The load was not that heavy, but it stood close to three feet above the roof. When we set out, we noticed that the wind resistance of the roof load could affect the steering of the car, but that didn't bother us as much as the nine miles per gallon we were getting. In Salt Lake City we shipped the roof load to Montgomery by train.

A few days later Dorothy and John welcomed us to their farm. Over the next couple of days, preparations were made by my family and other members of the farming community to have a wedding at the small country church Dorothy and John attended. In 1949 my mother made a wedding gown for Margie's wedding. Dorothy and Janice wore it in their weddings in 1952. Now, ten years later, it was prepared for Annelise to wear. Her family could not afford to come from Denmark for the wedding, so John, at age thirty-six, served as father of the bride. Until the day he died many years later, he would kid me by saying, "Giving Annelise away was the biggest mistake I ever made. Should've kept her for myself."

After the wedding and the reception provided by an older cousin, we drove south for an hour or two and stopped at a cheap motel in a small town. Annelise wanted to call her mother, so since our room had no telephone, we talked to the middle-aged lady in the office about a pay phone. When she learned we wanted to call the mother of the bride, she offered us her room. Annelise sat on her bed and talked to her mother in Denmark. As the call was costing $3.00 per minute, I paced the floor, looking at my watch. Today Annelise talks to her brother in Denmark for an hour at a time, on Skype, and it costs her nothing.

A Great Coincidence

WHEN DAVE AND I SPLIT up after our trip to Montgomery the year before, we lost touch. He went back to the state of Washington to live with his parents and go to college. One day while standing around with a group of fellow students, he happened to mention how much he enjoyed Panama City Beach, Florida, which was one of the places we visited. One of the young women in the group said that she too enjoyed visiting that beach.

They began talking and discovered that the young woman was Willa Henry Boozer, who had grown up a few houses down the road from my family in Montgomery. They began dating and fell in love. I didn't know anything about this romance and learned of their wedding plans only when I saw the engagement notice only a few inches away from our wedding notice in the nuptials section of the Montgomery paper.

I got in touch with Dave, and only a week or so after Annelise and I married in the small Snowdoun Methodist church out in the country, we attended their wedding in the large First Methodist Church in the city.

Married Student Life At Auburn

JANICE AND DAN CAME FROM California for our wedding, and they had crossed the country pulling their horse in a trailer. Following our three-day honeymoon in Florida, we loaded all our possessions, and Richard's, into the horse trailer and led Dan and Janice to the little house we had rented in Auburn, Alabama. Richard had also been accepted at Auburn and would live with us. The house had been a beauty shop at one time, which accounted for each room having a different color. We took the bedroom, and Richard got a fold-out bed in the breakfast nook.

Soon after we moved in and got settled, which didn't take long with so little to settle, Annelise secured a job with the Animal Sciences division of the university. She would drive the Comet, and I would ride the three-speed bicycle I bought at Western Auto.

A nursing home a few blocks away from the house was a good place for me to use my orderly experience, but when I applied they told me they hired only "colored people." I then checked with the university and secured a temporary job with the College of Agriculture. They paid me ninety cents an hour to count and package peas and corn kernels from experimental crops.

In the house next door lived a widower, a retired preacher who had served as a chaplain during the First World War. At that time he was in his eighties. Reverend Jones subscribed to the local newspaper, and each morning when he was through reading the paper he took it over and put it on our welcome mat. If we didn't pick it up by 8:00 a.m. or so, he would call and remind us it was there. Occasionally I would sit with him on his front porch and talk.

At this time the civil rights struggle was hot, and Rev. Jones hated the Kennedys for their support of Dr. King. On one occasion when we were talking, he got so angry that he sputtered, "Those Kennedys should be forced to eat boiled nigger!!!" While on this subject of race relations, he told me about going to the veterans hospital and getting a black veteran as a roommate. He said that when the man walked into

90

the room, he told him to get out. When the black man hesitated, the reverend hit him on the head with his cane.

The last time we saw Rev. Jones was after we had moved into student housing some months later. I picked him up and brought him over for supper. Annelise fixed meatloaf. After the meal he said, "Honey, that was the best steak I've ever eaten. It was so tender!"

Earlier that year, 1963, I applied for a National Defense Education Act (NDEA) loan and received $450, to be used to pay the $75 tuition each quarter. Since I had decided to major in education, I knew that the government would forgive up to half of the loan if I taught in poor schools. The following May I joined the Naval Reserve in Columbus, Georgia, thirty miles away, which paid $33 for one weekend a month of training. That amount covered our monthly rent in student housing.

One day when Annelise was in the neighboring city of Opelika, she happened to meet Sonya, a Danish woman her age. She was married to a German, Heinz, who had come to Opelika from Germany for a business opportunity. She called Heinz "my little Nazi." Sonya was close to delivering a baby and Heinz' business arrangement had fallen through.

After the baby was born, we took the couple, their baby, and their cat into our small, one-bedroom apartment in a triplex. They slept on the pull-out sofa bed, the baby slept in the closet, and the cat stayed inside and out. Heinz got work in Atlanta and came home on weekends. He hired a black woman to babysit the baby and do some housework while Sonya worked full time at the university.

Somebody from the student housing authority called one day to tell us we were not allowed to have the cat they saw coming out of our unit. That problem was greatly compounded when they learned that another couple and a baby were living there. Fortunately, by then Heinz and Sonya had saved enough money to pay their way back to Germany.

Auburn Football in the Early Sixties

ONLY ABOUT A HUNDRED YARDS away from Graves student housing was the football stadium. In the early sixties the students were expected to dress up for the games. The men wore coat and tie if the weather was cool and just shirt and tie if it was warm. The women wore a "dressy dress" and a chrysanthemum corsage. Although we married students looked like young ladies and gentlemen, we could get boisterous in the stands, especially in big games.

What helped make us boisterous was the bourbon we smuggled into the stadium to be mixed with the Coke we could buy there. A favorite way to smuggle the booze was to put it in an empty bottle or jar of some kind of liquid product women carried with them. All gate guards were young men who had no clue what women carried in their purses. Neither did their husbands for that matter. So Annelise was never asked to open her purse.

One significant characteristic of those football games was that the students could get in for $2.00 a ticket, and they could buy any ticket they wanted, even those for the very big games like the one against the University of Alabama (Joe Namath was the quarterback then). Another even more significant feature was that there were no black players because there were no black students. Another reason was the widespread belief among white boys and men, including me, that black men could not play serious football.

Graduation and the Gulf
of Tonkin Resolution

IN DECEMBER, 1964, I COMPLETED my coursework and student teaching. The graduation ceremony would be held in about a week, and I had one more reserve meeting to attend in Columbus. A notice came in the mail informing me that I was on standby to report to the Mayport Naval Station in Jacksonville, Florida. Congress had passed the Gulf of Tonkin Resolution and all armed services personnel were to stand by for mobilization orders. By then I had four years active duty and eighteen months active reserve, so I resigned from military service. Had I been subject to the mobilization, there was an excellent chance I would have been sent to Vietnam as a medic for the Marine infantry.

A few weeks earlier I had secured a job teaching English in the small town of LaBelle, Florida, so after graduation we loaded up a U-Haul trailer and pulled it to the farm. As we had very little money, John graciously co-signed a loan with us for $500. A day or two after New Year's Day, 1965, we got up in the dark one cold, rainy morning for our trip to LaBelle. We had parked in the pasture close to the house, and we got stuck. With Annelise at the wheel while I pushed, we reached the gravel driveway and were on our way. For the next fourteen hours we drove south while our small car and trailer were buffeted by the northerly winds bringing the bad weather.

Launching a Career in Labelle

THE HIGH SCHOOL PRINCIPAL HAD obtained a little house for us, and when we arrived we discovered it had only three doors—front, back and bathroom. We started unloading the car, and in the middle of our work Annelise leaned against the kitchen sink and started crying. I consoled her until we could resume unloading

Later, while considering what might have caused her breakdown, I realized that the change in her life over the previous three years must have been traumatic. In the San Francisco Bay area she was living quite well. She had even dated a man who drove a Morgan. Now she was married to a man who had courted her in his brother's '51 Studebaker, who had had to borrow $500 in order to start his career, and who had brought her to the edge of the Everglades to live in a small house with only three doors.

We had a 21" TV we had brought from California, and the next morning I attached one end of a lengthy TV cable to the back. I pushed the other end under the window screen and pulled the cable out into the yard. I attached that end to an aluminum yard chair and threw the chair up on the roof. When I turned on the TV I was able to pull in a pretty good picture from Channel 11 in Fort Myers, thirty miles away on the Gulf coast.

A day or two later, I introduced myself to my eleventh grade homeroom. Ten seconds into the introduction, one of the boys leaped over a couple of other students and slugged another boy, so my very first duty was to break up a fight. I soon learned that to maintain order we were allowed to paddle male students, but another teacher had to observe the paddling. I decided that was an improvement over the policy used at Cloverdale School. The terms of my contract were that for my $4500 annual salary I would teach 180 students in 7th, 8th, 11th, and 12th grades, plus maintain a homeroom class and be the faculty advisor for the eleventh grade. A few days before my first payday in February, we were down to our last fifty cents. To augment our remaining food, I did a little fishing in streams feeding the Caloosahatchee River nearby.

When payday finally arrived, I was told that I couldn't receive my paycheck until I joined the credit union, which required a five-dollar deposit. My principal was kind enough to lend me the money so I could get paid.

Yes, She Has No Bananas

ANNELISE'S BREAKDOWN WHILE WE WERE moving into our little house was the first of only a very few times she has cried during our fifty-year marriage. The rigors of her early life prepared her to be a strong, independent woman.

The day she was born, her father had to stay overnight in the maternity ward because of a curfew. Her home country of Denmark had been recently occupied by the German army. Even after the war and the German withdrawal, the Danish people still could not get many goods. Sweden had been neutral, so the Swedes had been able to get many things the Danes could not.

One day when she was five, her mother, Agnes, her brother Ole and she made a trip to Sweden to shop for those wonderful things they could now buy, provided they could get them through Swedish customs. After buying several sets of underwear for Annelise and Ole, Agnes took her children to a nearby park where she had them get behind a bush and put on all of the underwear under their clothes. She then took her two chubby children to the grocery store to buy food she couldn't get in Copenhagen.

At the customs office Agnes had to put her goods on the counter for the inspection of a rather rude and abrupt official. When the inspector refused to let her have a partially eaten container of butter, she got angry and shoved a partially eaten loaf of bread at him and said, "Well, then, just take the bread, too!" Annelise, who could barely reach the countertop, had been absentmindedly pushing along a coconut with her right hand while holding a bunch of bananas with her left hand. When the inspector saw the coconut he grabbed it and said she couldn't have it.

Agnes tried to tell him that the girl had never tasted or even seen a coconut before, but he didn't care. Annelise was afraid he would see her bananas and take them away also, so she put them behind her back and quietly slipped behind her mother and out of his sight. She wanted to be sure that she brought the bananas home to her father, who needed them for his stomach problems. Unseen in the mass of adults passing through the gate to board the ferry, she succeeded in getting the contraband bananas out of Sweden and into the hands of her beloved *Farman* (Daddy).

Annelise and Ole

Annelise and the Candy Factory

SHORTLY AFTER THE BANANA ESCAPADE, Annelise had to be hospitalized with a leg infection. She was put in a women's ward, and all of the women there spoiled her with constant attention. When she came home she wanted more sympathy and attention, so her mother invited Annelise's boyfriend Peter to come over and keep her company.

Peter, a handsome boy, was the perfect companion for Annelise. He not only gave her sympathy and attention but brought her a big bag of assorted candies. Peter's grandfather owned a candy factory. It's hard to imagine a more ideal boyfriend for a six-year-old girl than a good looking, attentive boy whose grandfather owns a candy factory.

George Walker: Great American

IN MARCH, 1965, TWO IMPORTANT events occurred. My hometown of Montgomery was again embroiled in racial strife. The small city of Selma became an international focal point for the Selma to Montgomery voting rights march. To my knowledge, none of my family or friends joined in the demonstrations against the marchers, but the beatings on the Edmund Pettus Bridge over the Alabama River and the murder of activist Viola Liuzza have made the name "Selma" synonymous with racial hatred.

The second event was meeting a fellow faculty member named George Jennings, later Walker. I first met George at a high school basketball game at LaBelle High School. He was sitting in the bleachers faking an interest in the game. I too was faking interest. Attending basketball matches was an obligation of our employment. We struck up a conversation at the game, conversed in the teachers' lounge later that week, and soon developed a friendship.

In addition to attending basketball games, we had to live in the school district so that our salaries would be spent at the local businesses. An unspoken requirement was that we go to church on Sundays. I had been baptized a Methodist but didn't attend church. George tried to pass himself off as a Buddhist, but they wouldn't accept that designation on the employment papers.

Another "requirement" was that the men faculty buy the principal's beer so he wouldn't be caught buying it himself. George and I didn't mind buying the beer, but we didn't like having to go to church every Sunday. We developed the habit of sleeping late then dressing up in suit and tie for a trip to Flo and El's sandwich shop, the local hangout, about noon for coffee and the newspaper. Our objective was to appear as though we had dropped by after church.

George was ten years older than I and had married his ex-landlady in Tallahassee a couple of years before. It was his first marriage and her third. Short with flaming red hair, Rita was ten years older than he and a devout Catholic. He was a devout atheist, yet they got along quite well. She had dropped him off in LaBelle on her way to a secretarial job in Miami. He took the Labelle job because he badly needed income, having just completed a master's in political science at Florida State University.

In LaBelle he lived in a one-room building behind the house of the school secretary, and he cooked his meals on a hotplate. Even though the town was small, he had some difficulty getting around on foot, so I lent him my bicycle. Being a talented freeloader, he would often show up at our tiny house just in time for supper. Annelise would look out the window at this figure on a bicycle weaving along the dirt road and say, "Here comes that man again." But you couldn't help liking George. Even though he was homely and short, his easygoing manner and quick, boisterous laugh endeared him to everybody. He was intelligent and well informed about local and national politics. He called both friend and foe "Great American." George served in WWII as a teenager but saw no justification for the Vietnam War. He said he would be glad to serve in Vietnam if he could hit the beach right behind President Lyndon Johnson and Secretary of Defense Robert McNamara.

After the school year ended, I moved on to another town to teach, and George accepted a job teaching at a military school in Miami near his wife's job. "Captain Jennings" lasted only one year. By the fall of 1966 they were back in Tallahassee, a city they loved. While in graduate school at FSU, George had run for mayor with the slogan, "Vote for the man who thinks like you do!" His entire campaign fund was spent on a haircut. His tactic to "split the vote" between the conservative and liberal candidates was a disaster, but he had a great time trying.

George and Rita drove a Renault. Why they liked that car was a head-scratching mystery, as it always needed repair. It was little more than a tin can with wheels. Rita told us that George would sometimes drive into a mall parking lot to turn around but would just keep turning in circles until she screamed "George!" While driving on the highway, he would close the eye she could see and begin nodding until she would jab him and he would start laughing.

We occasionally visited them in Tallahassee, where they lived in a nice, older section of the city. Rita had a good secretarial job, and George had secured a position with the Florida Department of Education. Even though Rita was an excellent cook, they took all of their meals at the local Frisch's Big Boy. George said they used the racks in the oven for storing books.

At Frisch's George would hold court over a coterie of coffee drinkers who discussed world problems for hours. When George and Rita weren't at work they were at Frisch's. In fact, they spent so much time and money there they got a monthly bill in the mail. In our address book we had both their home phone number and the number for Frisch's.

The years went by, I completed graduate school at the University of Florida, and George said I was one of those doctors who don't do you any good, alluding to the Ph.D. bureaucrats he worked with. George was a deeply caring person who sincerely wanted the best for the children but didn't think they had any chance of getting a good education from the state educational bureaucracy. He tempered his criticism of the system just enough to keep from getting fired. But he wasn't always careful. He told me they once asked him to say the blessing at an office picnic and he intoned, "God is great. God is good. Let us thank him for the fud."

Over the years, wherever we were living at the time, Rita always needed to know where the closest Catholic Church was before they could visit. I would locate the church and draw a map of how to get there. While she was gone, George and I would drink coffee and discuss global issues.

At some point along the way George had his name officially changed from Jennings to Walker to make himself more appealing as an heir to his rich, older, childless half-brother. Their mother had children by both a Walker and then a Jennings, but the Jennings side was much poorer, so George tried to cultivate his half-brother's interest in him by changing his name to Walker. But the tactic failed.

The only thing George loved more than drinking coffee was smoking cigarettes. Both he and Rita were heavy smokers—several packs a day each. George admitted that the cigarettes would probably kill him someday, and he was right. In 1990 he was sixty-two years old and had just retired from the state department. Concerned about some persistent pains in his stomach, he consulted one of those doctors "who can do you some good" and learned he had cancer throughout his stomach and chest.

Ever the fatalist, George made light of his plight when he discovered there was nothing to be done. I called him shortly after getting word of his illness, and he just asked if I called to have a final word with him.

A few weeks later Rita called to say he was gone. She also said that she wanted to have a religious service for him, but he said that if she had such a service he would come back and haunt her. In keeping with his wishes his body was cremated without ceremony and his ashes scattered in the woods. Rita died a year later.

As I observe the political strife in America today, I sometimes think of George and try to imagine the conversations he would be having with his pals at Frisch's. Coffee cup in one hand and cigarette in the other, he would be in his element, spreading his gospel, laughing, and perhaps turning the head of another young man susceptible to the intellectual and personality force of George Walker, Great American.

Teaching Whites, Blacks and Reds (Seminoles)

AS THERE WERE NO JOBS available for Annelise in LaBelle, she had a lot of time on her hands. Then one day she got a knock on the door from a public health nurse who said she had heard that Annelise was a lab tech, and two doctors were looking for a lab/x-ray tech. She took the job, and we rented a more conventional house close to the hospital where she would work in the neighboring city of Clewiston, thirty miles away. I learned that I could get a job teaching at Clewiston High School the next school year.

For the next few months I commuted from Clewiston to LaBelle. One day I was a little late getting away from home and was speeding down the long, flat highway when I came upon a roadblock. The police aircraft had clocked my speed between two lines on the pavement at eighty-three miles per hour. I was escorted to LaBelle, the county seat, where I was taken directly to the jail. A couple of other men and I stood outside the jail cell while trying to arrange bail over the phone. I called my principal, who vouched to the arresting officers that I was trustworthy to report to court when called.

When the school year ended, I taught summer school and worked as a janitor doing maintenance work on the school building and grounds. These jobs gave us a little more income to make the move with. In the middle of August I reported to the faculty orientation session at the high school. The school facilities there were better than those at LaBelle, and I had to teach only the eleventh and twelfth grades. I got the additional challenge of teaching Seminole Indians in senior English. The curriculum called for English literature, but since their language skills were quite weak I had them sit in a back corner and do language exercises in workbooks for part of the week.

I was told that only two Seminoles had graduated from high school, and only one of those had graduated from college. That following summer another teacher and I took jobs with the Bureau of Indian Affairs on Big Cypress reservation, where we learned, because of cultural and historical differences, that the integration of the "red" man into white society would be more difficult than integrating the black. For example, one of the tribal leaders told me that one day in the fall of 1928, the Seminoles studied the behavior of insects and animals and concluded that a hurricane was headed their way, so they packed up and went deep into the Everglades without telling the white people.

Clewiston is at the southern end of Lake Okeechobee. The hurricane came ashore on the Atlantic coast, moved westward onto the lake, and headed south. The water and wind that swept ashore in Clewiston and other communities destroyed huge swaths of property south of the lake and killed almost 3000 people.

Black-white relations in Clewiston were the same as they were in Montgomery. Not even the principal of the black high school was entitled to be called "Mister." Everyone referred to him as "Amos." But "the times they were a-changing," and pressure was building to integrate the schools. At the beginning of the second semester I was given the job of admitting two black boys to my eleventh grade English class. Those two bright, well-dressed young men took the first two seats inside the classroom. None of the white students took seats in the rest of that row or in the row next to that one. I said nothing, and in a matter of a week or so the empty seats filled, and the tension passed.

The Big Cypress Seminole reservation was forty miles into the Everglades. In the summer of 1966, on our way back and forth to our teaching jobs there, my colleague and I discussed graduate school. I had never considered a master's or doctorate, but he had, and he convinced me to apply for admission.

Even though both of us had served in the military prior to completing college, neither of us had been eligible for the G.I. Bill, which had expired after the Korean War. Now the Vietnam War was heating up and the Bill was re-implemented and made retro-active to include the time we had served. After almost two years of teaching at the high school level, the prospect of teaching college was quite appealing, so I applied for admission to the College of Arts and Sciences at the University of Florida to work on a master's degree in English and was accepted.

While I was finishing summer school at the reservation, Richard came down for a visit, and he and Annelise made a trip up to Gainesville to arrange housing for us. They bought a new 12 X 60 mobile home and had it pulled to the OK Trailer Park southwest of the campus.

The Anglo-Saxons

IN SEPTEMBER I BEGAN WORK on a master's in English while teaching freshman English as a graduate assistant. In the middle of October, some of the advanced graduate students began wearing black armbands around campus. When I asked about the sad occasion, I was told that the Anglo-Saxons were defeated by the Norman French at the Battle of Hastings on October 14, 1066, exactly 900 years ago. When I asked why that was a sad event, they explained that the victorious Normans imposed an inferior language and culture on the Anglo-Saxon people. I was of course devastated by the news.

Six months later, soon after the spring term began, the English department in Anderson Hall announced a date for the master's exam. That's when I experienced temporary insanity. I set a goal to pass the exam even though I had not taken enough courses, having done my bachelor's degree in English Education. My plan for passing the exam was to read seven hours a day (not counting breaks), seven days a week, for the seven weeks until the exam. We would be tested on two thousand years of literature—British, American, and some European and Asian.

My routine was to read for an hour, take a ten-minute break, and read for another hour. I did this until the seven hours were completed, which could take ten to fourteen hours a day. I made the mistake of sitting on a hard chair in the second bedroom of our trailer. Toward the end of my 343-hour study ordeal, my rear end began to complain. The night before the exam I went to the drugstore and bought a tube of Preparation H. From time to time over my teaching career I told my students that I literally "broke my ass" to get through college. My grade on the exam was Low Pass.

In addition to the coursework, the master's exam, and the foreign language exam, we also wrote a master's thesis. One of my professors was Dr. Paul Thurston, who held the Chaucer chair at the university. I took two courses from him, enough to become fairly fluent in Chaucerian English. He agreed to supervise my thesis, and over the next year I worked on the paper while I taught reading at Lincoln High School, the junior-senior high school for black students in Gainesville. I was one of two white teachers on the faculty. That year of teaching while working on the thesis was complicated by a state-wide strike called by the Florida Education Association, to which I belonged.

The Normans

IN THE FALL OF 1967, even though I hadn't yet completed the M.A. degree in the College of Arts and Sciences, I applied to graduate school in the College of Education in Norman Hall. I had developed an interest in community colleges, which were springing up all over the country. Their main appeal was that they offered only the first two years of college and specialized in remediation, tutoring services, and faculty-student conferences.

The large numbers of these colleges meant that hundreds of thousands of entering freshman could complete the first two years of college while living at home. In Florida the goal was to locate a community college within fifty miles of any resident. If such a college had been available to me, I would have had a much better chance of finishing once I started. I could have completed an Associate of Arts degree at a community college close to home then transferred to Alabama as a junior.

The Labor Break

IN THE SPRING OF 1969 I received my M.A. degree from Arts and Sciences and decided to take the following summer off. I went to the double-wide mobile home of the owner of our park and asked if he had a summer job I could do. Over the previous three years, OK Trailer Park had become Westgate Mobile Manor with the addition of enough spaces to triple the size of the park. All of that extra construction meant job opportunities.

When I asked him for a job, he got a very puzzled look on his face. He asked about my heart condition. I told him I did not have any health problems and asked how he got that idea. He said that the lights in my trailer were on all night and that Annelise drove our car when we went out, so the rumor started that I had a heart problem. Despite my assuring him that I was in very good health, he did not hire me.

Upon discussing this with Annelise, we decided the community had drawn a false conclusion from the evidence. They didn't see much of me because I spent most of my time studying. They saw the lights late at night because I liked to study late at night. They saw me being driven because Annelise dropped me off on her way to her lab job at the medical school.

A day or two later I learned from another student in the park about the laborers union in Gainesville. He and I applied for membership, paid our modest dues and secured jobs on a fairly regular basis over that summer. My jobs involved working at one or another construction site in Gainesville, as the university was growing fast during those years. I swept floors, pushed wheelbarrows of wet concrete, and assisted various skilled craftsmen. I very much enjoyed working only with my hands rather than my head.

On one job I should have stuck to using just my hands, but during our lunch break my first day on the job I discussed the Vietnam conflict with the other workers. I thought we had had an enjoyable, engaging discussion, but not too long after we went back to work the foreman came over, gave me a few dollars and told me he didn't need me anymore.

Moon Struck

IN JULY OF THAT YEAR we took a trip to Crescent Beach near St. Augustine with three other couples. We had a wonderful time staying in small clapboard cabins in an inlet next to the Atlantic Ocean. Just outside the front door of each cabin was an oyster bed where we gathered and feasted on oysters.

On our way home we were driving along a state highway when a car passed us. It must have been other college students because one of the men exposed his naked butt. I was quite surprised, not having seen that maneuver before. One of the guys in our car said that we were being "mooned." Now that I had been introduced to this cultural gem of college life, we pulled into the trailer park and parked in front of our trailer. All eight of us went inside, loaded up on beer and chips, and sat down on the sofa and floor to watch Neil Armstrong and Buzz Aldren land on the surface of the moon.

Finding a Home in Atlanta

OVER THE NEXT TWO YEARS in Gainesville, we managed comfortably on Annelise's salary and my G.I. Bill. I used the last of my G.I. benefits in the spring of 1971, so we paid for the final term out of pocket and I got my Doctor of Education in the mail at the end of August. Even before I received my diploma, we began preparing to move to Atlanta, where I had secured a faculty position at DeKalb College east of the city. We sold our trailer and loaded up a U-Haul truck with "all of our worldly possessions," which had grown some from the day we left California. Our car was a 1967 Saab, which was the size of a Volkswagen beetle. To save space, we drove the car into the truck, stuffed it with as much as we could, and packed all around it. We left in the wee hours one morning and arrived in Atlanta six hours later. Our new home was a two-bedroom apartment a short walk from the college campus. A few months later, when Annelise secured a job at a science lab at Emory University, a few miles west, she drove to her job, and I walked to mine.

Carsten Bo Joins Our Family

AFTER I GRADUATED FROM AUBURN, we began trying to have a baby. Upon arriving in Atlanta, almost seven years later, we were still trying. Soon after Annelise started working we gave up and put in for adoption. A couple of months later she became pregnant, so we canceled the application to adopt. The pregnancy was uneventful, and she delivered our son Carsten Bo on Veteran's Day, 1972.

The timing of the delivery was perfect for me. She woke me on a Saturday morning at about 7:00 a.m. to drive her to the hospital. I lounged about the hospital while she went through labor. Around 2:00 p.m., while I was watching the Alabama-LSU football game in the fathers' waiting room, the obstetrician rolled the baby into the room for me to see. I noted that he was the size and color of a football and nodded my approval. He was rolled away to the nursery and I got back to the game.

Carsten has proven to be a wonderful son. He has a nice, easy-going manner that makes him very popular with friends and business associates. When he was about two, I got a hint of his rosy outlook on life when I was scolding him for some minor offense. He looked up at me with sad eyes and protruding lower lip and said, "Daddy, you're making me sad."

When he was about twelve he discovered rock music. He got word that the rock band *Kiss* was coming to Atlanta and begged us to let him go. At the family celebration of my 70th birthday, in keeping with tradition, a family "gazette" was printed to share our memories of the birthday boy or girl. Below is Carsten's recollection of his first rock concert:

So I like heavy metal. Or I did back in 1984 when I was a wee lad of 12 years. I had lots of great heavy metal from bands like Quiet Riot, Krokus, Ozzy, and my personal favorite, Twisted Sister. These bands were raw, electrifying, and loud. They were the perfect soundtrack to my awkward, junior high existence. They also did crazy things during their performances. It was rumored that Ozzy would bite the heads off bats at his shows, or

112

drink a large cup of spit that had been collected by being passed around the audience. This I had to see in person. I found out about a truly epic show that was coming to Atlanta and I desperately wanted to go. It was KISS. KISS meant crazy makeup, pyrotechnics and fake blood. Ohhhhhh yes. I politely and respectfully asked my parents if they would consider purchasing me a ticket to this monumental show. They said no. No, no, no, no, no, no, no, despite my begging and pleading. They thought KISS might be a little too crazy for my tender eyes. This was bad, bad news, but it had a silver lining. They felt bad. They wanted me to go see a show, just not that one.

So, with a stroke of good luck, they promised me that I could go to the very first show I wanted to see. This proved to be very fortuitous for me because about six months later the holy grail of metal in my mind was coming to town. Twisted Sister. They would be opening up for Iron Maiden at the Omni in Atlanta. I excitedly told my parents about it and they agreed to take my friend Kevin and me to the show. Mom drew the short straw and would be the one chaperoning us, along with Charlie, Kevin's dad. The day of the show finally arrived and mom wasn't feeling well. I'm not sure if she was truly sick or just sick at the thought of having to go to the show, but this meant that dad would be taking over the chaperoning duty. Dad does not like Heavy Metal. Dad, who considers Hall & Oates too heavy, much prefers the gaiety of a sing-a-long in a Rodgers and Hammerstein musical. Now he would have to sit through three hours of earsplitting electric guitar and thunderous drum solo's. It's probably the last place on earth he would want to be.

Regardless, he was ready for the challenge and dressed up in his coolest shirt, jeans and sunglasses. We picked up Kevin and Charlie and headed for the Omni. The scene was electric as we made our way to our seats in the nosebleed section. The house lights went down and people all around us started lighting up funny looking cigarettes. Twisted Sister took the stage and blasted my eyeballs out of my skull. This was truly radical and I was in Heaven. Iron Maiden came on next with their mascot, Eddie, a 20 foot tall zombie/skeleton and continued the mayhem. I don't know if it was the questionable air quality or the late hour but eventually I fell asleep. I probably dreamed of all the cool things I could tell my friends at school the next day. One of my favorite questions I like to ask people is what their first concert was. Lots of people respond with something lame like New Kids on the Block or ABBA, but thanks to my dad I can proudly say that at my first show I got my face melted by Twisted Sister and Iron Maiden. Thanks dad. Happy birthday, I love you, and YOU ROCK!

Carsten and Harris on their way to the rock concert

Plastic Ivy

DeKalb was starting its eighth year when I began teaching there in the fall of 1971. I soon learned that it had high academic standards. I even heard the self-congratulatory term "Harvard of community colleges" being used This prompted some of the wags in the English Department to say that our status in the Ivy League would require that our ivy be made out of plastic. However, the derogatory remarks were not meant to be disparaging, for the faculty was indeed committed to high standards for our academically weaker student body.

Our students were weaker because most were not traditional "college material." The college had an "open door" admission policy which admitted any high school graduate. Those academically weak, as shown by the ACT or SAT, together with in-house placement instruments, would be enrolled in remedial courses in math, reading and English. The weakest of our students could spend the first year completing remedial courses—longer if they failed any of them. We constructed syllabi for our courses that placed a heavy burden on both the students and ourselves. I graded student papers every weekend during the term.

In those early years, from time to time a student would tell me that if he didn't pass my class he would lose his student deferment from the Vietnam War draft. I told him to try harder and to come to my office for counseling. Unlike universities, where undergraduate students rarely confer with professors, our community college required us to post conference hours for every day or night we taught.

Becoming a College Administrator

DURING THE SPRING QUARTER OF my first year, I was called to the president's office to be interviewed for an administrative position at the second campus, to be opened the next fall. I was selected to be Head of the Humanities/Fine Arts Division. In addition to teaching a full class load, my duties were to supervise and facilitate the work of thirteen faculty members with the assistance of a division secretary and a few student assistants. For my administrative duties I was paid an additional $750/year. My total compensation was about $12,000/year plus what I could earn teaching classes during the summer term.

As Division Chair I encouraged my faculty to launch non-traditional projects as ways to facilitate the learning of our non-traditional students. Our reading teacher Pat York set up a reading lab, the first for the college. This led to a variety of learning labs and eventually computer labs. The English faculty implemented inter-disciplinary courses of various kinds. The most memorable involved the participation of our academic dean, Marvin Cole.

Mark Twain Comes to DeKalb College

THIS PARTICULAR INTERDISCIPLINARY COURSE MERGED English 101, Psychology 101 and History 101. The three courses were given a three-hour block of time, which meant that a single course could sometimes be given all three hours. One of the extended English activities was to have the 70-80 students interview a panel of faculty members about the assigned novel, *Huckleberry Finn*. The English instructor, Agnes Donaldson, invited Marvin Cole to sit on the panel. Marvin was (and is) a most agreeable, obliging colleague/administrator, so he agreed to re-read the book and serve on the panel.

Marvin's experience on that panel changed his life. He developed a keen interest in Mark Twain's life and work. He said the novel was not the same one he read as a boy. Some of the English faculty told him he resembled Twain and should consider becoming an impersonator like Hal Holbrook. He recently told me that he almost dropped out of college because of his fear of a required speech course. But he took on the challenge. I can still see Marvin and his secretary, Katherine, walking from the administration building to the gym so he could practice onstage. Katherine was a theater major. Without neglecting his administrative duties, Marvin dedicated himself to becoming a Twain impersonator.

He began getting invitations to perform at colleges and grade schools and civic organizations. This led to being invited to appear at business and professional conferences. He charges little or nothing for appearances at non-profits but charges a range of fees for other groups. He has performed from coast to coast and on a few paddlewheel boats on the Mississippi River. Overall he has lost much more money than he has made, he says. His reward has been the performing itself, the many accolades he has received, and his changed outlook on life.

I have seen his show many times, but because he has over six hours of material committed to memory I have never seen the same show twice. In 1994 he retired as president of DeKalb College but continues his work as a Twain impersonator. Now in his early eighties, Marvin still practices, still performs, still incorporates new material into his act.

The Day the Educators Got "Stung"

IN ADDITION TO THEIR TEACHING and counselling duties, each year the faculty were required to serve on one or two college committees. One year, we on the Faculty Development Committee got quite creative. At our initial meeting in the fall, while discussing what we might do to "develop" the faculty, we found ourselves in a mischievous mood and decided that rather than prepare the usual program we would spoof the consultants who traveled from college to college dispensing expertise.

The "plot" involved Agnes (our chairman), Bob, Wayne, and me. For the next few months we congregated in one member's office or the other and spent the whole time laughing, sometimes uproariously. In fact, we were afraid we were going to spill the beans if we weren't more careful. Fortunately, nobody suspected anything and the plot thickened.

We decided to create an outrageous "consultant." Bob's brother-in-law, Andy, had majored in drama but was working at a nearby plastics plant. Andy agreed to play the role, and we decided to have him speak on Faculty Development Day. The first thing we did was to create an impressive *curriculum vitae* for "Dr. Justice." He was to speak to the full faculty and administration in the library as the crowning event of the day. We formed a panel made up of the committee, whose job would be to ask the expert questions, taking turns.

Our "expert" would stand at a lectern next to the panel and respond to each question. Of course everything was rehearsed, and he knew all of the questions beforehand, but we pretended the answers were spontaneous. One ticklish problem we had to deal with was arranging the "honorarium" for our speaker. Would it be fraud to ask for money under these circumstances? Our "Ph.D. in educational administration" had a bachelor's in theater. Agnes handled the problem, and I don't know what she did, but I'm convinced that no one other than the committee knew of our plan.

The questions we picked were those of particular interest to our colleagues. The first answers were compatible with their views, but the later ones were less so as the session continued. We on the panel were facing the audience, so it was priceless to watch their expressions as they listened to the increasingly more outrageous answers. One faculty member scribbled furiously on her pad, as she prepared for the Q&A.

Toward the end, the following question was asked: "What can a college administrator do to further the professional growth of his/her faculty?" The answer was something like, "Mainly stay out of their way. Our research shows that the more administrators do to help their faculty the more they hurt them. Our advice is to eliminate most meetings, stop giving the faculty inane paperwork, and so forth. We find that most administrators are mainly concerned about advancing their own careers."

With that, one of our deans jumped up from his chair and yelled, "Not THIS administrator!" and sat down. At this point the audience began getting restless and muttering to each other, so the speaker stopped talking. Over the intercom, quietly at first then increasingly louder, came the theme song from the Paul Newman and Robert Redford movie "The Sting." Soon the audience caught on to the message of the music and realized they had been stung.

As we mingled with our colleagues, we discovered that with the exception of one or two, everyone enjoyed our "program." Even though the whole thing was a ruse, we felt it was one of the best programs ever presented since it "dramatically" taught two valuable lessons: Not all "expert" advice is worthwhile, and maybe we shouldn't be so interested in expert advice anyway. As for me, it was the most enjoyable committee duty I ever had.

My Life as a Recovering Racist

MY LIFE AS A RECOVERING racist began that night sixty years ago when I hit the old black man with the water balloon. My recovery continued when I experienced the reaction of the white adults to the Bus Boycott. Racial segregation in the armed forces was abolished in 1947, so when I joined the military in 1957 I served alongside sailors and Marines of all races. One of my superior officers was black. On Hotel Street in Honolulu, among many Asians and Hawaiians, I got a taste of what it's like to be in a racial minority.

By the time I started teaching at DeKalb College, affirmative action was in force, and while serving as an administrator I hired a black teacher for our then all-white faculty on the South Campus. She went on to have a distinguished career at the college. An increasing number of our students were black, and like our student body in general they were admitted under our "open door" policy. As a teacher of those students I made the most progress in my "recovery."

A high percentage of our black students had to take the remedial classes, and the temptation to "give them slack" was strong. I decided early on that to lower standards for them because they were suffering from the effects of racism was a form of racism itself. My position was and still is that all students must be held to the same standards but some must be given extra assistance to meet those standards. To do otherwise is fraud and discrimination. If a student just cannot meet the standards for whatever reason, he or she must be put into another curriculum. My status as a white man from Alabama caused me very few problems during my teaching career. With very few exceptions, my black students understood that I was hard on them because I cared about them.

Life after Retirement

AFTER MANY YEARS OF CHALLENGING but satisfying work, I was able to retire in order to pursue an interest in what I call "recreational education." I have either taught or arranged to be taught a wide range of subjects to retirees. They range from cooking classes to the geological history of the Appalachian Mountains.

Writing is my main post-retirement activity. In 2000 I co-authored *Our Finest Hour: the Way We Were in WWII,* a musical/theatrical tribute to the "greatest generation." I play the part of a history professor who relates the most significant historical and cultural events between 1940 and 1945, and my co-author Alan Gibson plays a Walter Winchell type newscaster who gives dramatic immediacy to the events I speak about. We sit on opposite sides of the stage, and between us onstage the lives of two young soldiers and two young USO volunteers unfold. The drama is musically enriched by a combo of USO musicians backing an Andrew Sisters type trio and a Big Crosby type baritone.

In 2006, as a member of the Big Canoe Writers club, I published *Chinaberry Summer: Riverton, Alabama 1947,* a novel inspired by that wonderful summer when I wore nothing but short pants and had nothing but the occasional nickel or dime. I remember buying a Popsicle for a nickel when I wished I had a dime for the Eskimo Pie. What I had plenty of was unlimited free time and a rich imagination.

At the back of this book is a Supplement section containing a poem and a few letters, essays and short stories. Most of them have been published, two of them nationally. Below is a Valentine I wrote for Annelise a few years ago:

Annelise,

In fall nineteen sixty-one
You became the only one.
Cupid shot me in the heart.
Told me we would never part.
This crude card is mighty fine.
I saved a buck ninety-nine.

Love,
Harris

Annelise was able to retire two years after I did. She enjoys performing her role of *Farmor* (Danish for "father's mother") of our granddaughter Harper. Carsten and his business partner Jonathan McIntyre own The Midway Pub in Atlanta. The pub was recently selected as one of the hundred best sports bars in the United States by CNN Travel. I told Carsten that I would be pleased to read poetry to his customers. His response to my offer was that he would like for me to read at 2:45 a.m., fifteen minutes after "last call."

Carsten's wife Leigh, mother of Harper, recently took leave from her corporate executive job to care for Harper and help run the pub. During Annelise's lab tech career, she worked in a wide variety of jobs. The last one involved working with primates at the Yerkes Primate Center at Emory University in Atlanta. That experience has given her valuable preparation for dealing with the retired primate she is married to.

Today, as she has always done, she keeps our household running smoothly. Over the years, she has taken on jobs I wouldn't attempt, such as replacing the heating element in an electric oven and fixing a broken toilet. She uses me for chimpanzee-level unskilled labor such as yard work, vacuuming, cleaning bathrooms, etc.

Because I don't pay much attention to proper dress, she has begun marking my old clothes. She writes "Yard Pants" or "Yard Shirt" across the front to keep me from wearing them out in public. One day I kidded her that while I was teaching recently one of my students asked me what "Yard Pants" means.

We have always been tender-hearted toward creatures great and small, but in our old age we have become even more so, she especially.

For the last few years she has begun keeping a "bug cup" under the sink in the upstairs and downstairs bathrooms. Any "bug" she finds she gets her implements and traps it, including the spiders she dislikes. Then she takes it outside and sets it free. At first only she did that, but now she has me going for the bug cup.

Some mornings when I finish breakfast and start downstairs to my office, I tell her that if the President calls I'm downstairs. I make this remark when I want to give the current president some feedback, which is often. Other times when I start downstairs I just say it's time for me to <u>swing</u> into action. On days when I'm feeling especially energetic I say <u>spring</u> into action. If she asks me what my plans are for the day, I sometimes say I will be "thinking great thoughts."

One recent great thought is a BMI (Body/Mass/Index) restaurant. The guest is greeted by the hostess who has him or her step on a scale. The BMI score is then displayed on a large screen so the other guests can compare themselves to the new guest. The menus are color-coded, depending on one's score. The menu for the worst BMI score is bright red.

Another great idea is a combination golf course/cemetery. Given the high cost and small size of a burial plot, millions of dollars could be raised selling plots over a standard 400-acre golf course. The clubhouse would resemble a funeral home, and the golf carts would be black. The course would be closed on Mondays for maintenance and funerals. For an extra monthly fee, the tee and yardage markers could also be used as headstones for the deceased. For example, it could read, "Ed Klutz (1943-2015)" and underneath "137 yards."

When I express these thoughts, she just sighs and reminds herself that she is married to a man who fell out of a tree house and landed on his head.

Harris Green
Big Canoe, Georgia
August, 2013

Annelise and Harris celebrating their 51st anniversary

Supplement

Parody of a Poem

"Shopping to Buy Woods on a Snowy Evening"

(if Robert Frost had been a golfer)

Whose woods these are I think I know.
IIis handicap is very low;
He will not see me shopping here
To see his woods fill me with woe.

My little wife must think it queer
To shop without a club pro near
Between the woods and bunker rakes
The darkest evening of the year.

She gives her earring bells a shake
To ask if there is some mistake.
The only other sound's the sweep
Of many practice swings I take.

The woods are lovely, taut and cheap.
But I've a handicap to keep,
And smiles to give so I won't weep,
And smiles to give so I won't weep.

Letters
to the Editor

"The Barnyard of American Politics"

Dear Editor:

Having spent time in barnyards in my youth, I know how to walk carefully to avoid unpleasant matter attaching itself to the bottom of my shoes. Although I walk carefully through the barnyard of American politics, I still get sorry politicians stuck to the bottom of my shoes. Since we voters are stuck with "representatives" who have no term limits, I am restricted to voting them out of office. Therefore, each time I go to the polls I find a sharp, stout railing on the barnyard fence and carefully scrape them off my shoes.

"An Interstate Highway and a Virgin Forest"

Dear Editor:

After learning about the proposal to build an interstate highway from Savannah to Knoxville, I renewed my commitment to political contraception. Our "public servants" assure us that the proposed I-3 will relieve traffic around Atlanta and improve air quality. What are a few mountain peaks with their rich biodiversity and rare medicinal herbs compared to those lofty objectives?

The proposed interstate goes through Robbinsville, NC, a moist, cool refuge from flatland summer heat, where Snowbird Cherokee culture mixes easily with the Scotch-Irish in a quiet mountain village off the beaten path.

Nearby is the Joyce Kilmer Memorial Forest of virgin trees. Two miles away is the charming, stone-clad Snowbird Lodge, built back in the thirties to accommodate visitors to the newly created Forest.

Maybe the interstate highway could be brought in close to the lodge so that it is more accessible to motorists. The two-mile stretch between the lodge and the virgin forest would be perfect for motels, restaurants and shopping centers. The mountain road could be four-laned to facilitate access to the businesses.

Since the Joyce Kilmer Memorial Forest is named for the poet who wrote "Trees," maybe an animatronic tree outside the entrance could "lift its leafy arms to pray" to appeal to the religious right. The motel owners could attract the less religious with clever allusions to the "virgin" forest.

I can hardly wait.

"Welcome to Funsy U"

Dear Editor:

As a retired college professor, I am mystified by the current practice in "higher" education of elevating the prestige of the name of the institution while lowering its academic standards. Junior colleges are now colleges and colleges are now universities. One day soon universities will be—what—megaversities? Of course, traditional universities don't have time to worry about their names because they are totally committed to making the alumni happy by producing athletic championships by recruiting the right "scholar" athletes. If I ever win the lottery (which I would need to start playing), I will jump on the bandwagon and open Funsy U:

Welcome to Funsy U! Our mission is to make sure U have fUn all the time! We believe a young face looks much better smiling than frowning, so all of our classes are very easy! U come if you feel like it. If you get bored, just get Up and leave. Or stay and chat with that good looking girl or boy in the adjacent seat (adjacent means the next seat over—sorry!). No tests, no papers, none of that boring stuff. Promise! To make very sure that U enjoy our classes, our faculty members are called Funmakers. In some BORING universities they are called professors. But at Funsy U, where college is a blast, the Funmakers, upon request, will dance, sing, juggle, do magic tricks, imitate animals, etc. for your amusement. You want to make a You-Tube video of the antics? No problem. If you find the performance especially enjoyable you can put something in the tip jar on his or her desk.

With the current financial persecution of schools and colleges with pernicious "furloughs," in which teachers and professors are obliged to work without pay, the need to make college fun has never been greater.

Non-fiction

"Find a Mutt to Love"

HOW MANY TIMES HAVE YOU driven past an emaciated mongrel dog standing next to the highway? Your heart goes out to the poor creature, but what can you do to help it? You probably can't help that particular dog, but you can help others by adopting a shelter dog and encouraging others to do the same.

First of all, shelter dogs are lovable, loving, and long-lived. You discover this upon entering the run and walking past their cages. With few exceptions, each dog is standing next to his gate, tongue lolling, eyes shining, seeming to say, "Pick me!" You know instinctively that any one of them would make a wonderful addition to a family, especially one with small children. You know that the dog would become a constant, protective companion for even the youngest of the children, always ready to chase a ball, take a walk, or share a nap. And you know that he would probably have a long life because, unlike their purebred counterparts, mongrels enjoy a "hybrid genetic vigor" that protects them from the injuries and diseases common to the pure breeds.

A second benefit of taking a shelter dog into your family is helping to eliminate the millions of unwanted dogs raiding garbage cans or joining dangerous dog packs. Too many of our fellow citizens are insensitive to the consequences of not caring for a family dog. They fall in love with a pretty puppy but reject the ugly dog it becomes. Some will chain the dog in the yard and use it as a watchdog. Others just let the dog run loose and if it doesn't get run over by a car or killed by a dog pack, it breeds more pretty puppies. It only takes three or four generations for two unwanted dogs to become hundreds. Of course, adopting just one animal does little more than make a statement, so you must also encourage others to adopt, and you must contribute money to or volunteer for community spay and neuter drives. In these ways you can take a bite out of the problem of unwanted and mistreated dogs.

In his 2008 victory speech, Barack Obama said he and Michelle would be giving their two daughters the puppy promised to them following the campaign. He said they would be looking at shelter dogs because, as a child of a black Kenyan father and a white American mother, he—like the shelter dogs—is a "mutt." Perhaps our "mutt" president will inspire us to make the population of unwanted American dogs so small that all of them can be adopted and loved.

"A View of Christo's 'The Gates' in New York City"

WE SHOULD VALUE CHRISTO'S LATEST ART project in New York City because it shines a critical light on American values. And rather than making its statement in an art gallery, "The Gates" is "in your face" all over Central Park.

It criticizes our values by being impractical. Deeply rooted in American culture is our pragmatism, our conviction that everything must serve a practical purpose. If something doesn't have utilitarian value, such as a shovel or a washing machine, it should at least be like rare coins or paintings and make money. "The Gates" serves no practical purpose other than perhaps making NYC a little tourist money via Mayor Bloomberg. Its very uselessness is part of its charm. It reminds us how very materialistic we are. We're told that Christo worked long and hard on various money making art projects in order to finance "The Gates." In other words, he labored to "waste" his money.

It is ephemeral. Even though it cost $21,000,000 and involved enormous political and physical effort to realize, the art will survive only a few weeks. Another important cultural tenet we Americans embrace is that things not only have practical value but last a long time. But like practicality, permanence is losing ground to profit-making and status. However, old habits die hard. Our sense of propriety is violated because "The Gates" is not only "useless" but will soon be gone.

The artwork is beautiful and evocative. These perfectly erect sentinels that overarch the walkways of Central Park express a kind of disciplined, regimented beauty. The gates are roughly akin to the guards at Buckingham Palace in that they offer ceremonial "protection" to those who pass beneath them. But rather than being rigidly masculine and militaristic in bearing, they are sensual and feminine in their soft, flowing, billowing, breeze-generated movement. The reddish pink color of the fabric adds to the effect. The red of Mars is subdued by

141

the pink of Venus. And we of a certain age are subtly reminded of the sheets hanging from our mothers' clotheslines. As children we loved to run into the sheets and let their cool dampness rake across our faces, as we passed beneath the line. The damp sheets exuded a delicious clean, sweet smell. We abandoned ourselves to the joy of running through the sheets. Our mothers worried about their sheets getting dirty.

"The Gates" is mythological. Once it's gone, leaving not a trace, it takes on a "once upon a time" and "I remember when" quality. Even young children will be able to tell younger children about the experience. Also, walking through the gates constitutes a kind of birthing activity, in which the person who emerges from them is different from the person who entered them. He walks through a kind of "tunnel," a passageway that carries him from here to there. In the same way that one cannot put his hand in the same stream twice, neither can he emerge from the gates as the same person he was when he entered. Psychologists would say that this is a common occurrence in everyday life, and is very common in ritual, as when we are baptized. But "The Gates" enhances the experience because passing through them, like baptism, is a special event. A primitive person brought to Central Park might assume the strollers passing through the gates are engaged in a rite of passage. He might be perplexed as to why they are not dressed in ceremonial garb or why they are of such varied ages. He would quickly see that the "ritual" is obviously not a passage into puberty or death and might conclude that it serves no "practical purpose."

Fiction

"The Lasher"

MABRY RUSSELL KNEW ONLY TOO well that he had no more than a fifty-fifty chance. But the alternative was almost unimaginable, so he had no choice, really. He had to go for it. He had to make a dash for freedom. The open area he had to cross was small—only about twenty feet—but the danger was hideous. A lasher about five feet in length sat nearby in brooding silence. He noticed it was female, even more dangerous than the male if there are young in the vicinity. A lasher in defense of her hatchlings is fury incarnate.

His situation was this: the lasher's back was turned toward him, but he would have to pass within forty feet of her. Could he be quiet enough to escape her preternatural sense of hearing? Having lived in this region for a number of years, Mabry was keenly aware of the awesome power of the lasher. He knew that their keen sense of hearing was more than matched by their uncanny eyesight and sense of smell, and that they strike with lightning speed over great distances—all of which made the bravest man sick with fear.

While carefully considering the magnitude of the danger he faced and weighing his chances, his dry throat made drier by the rivulets of sweat coursing down his face into his mouth, he became delirious and imagined himself standing at the edge of a clear jungle pool looking up at a thundering waterfall. Just as he envisioned himself gliding into the pool, in naked splendor, he snapped out of his reverie and sputtered, through clenched teeth, "Concentrate! Concentrate! For God's sake concentrate!"

He found himself clutching the club in his hands so tightly that his palms were stinging. And how stupid, he thought, to be holding such a puny weapon in the face of such horrible danger. All he could do was wait for some sign that the lasher might be asleep or at least distracted. After three or four minutes of agony, muscles tightened to the breaking point, sweat streaming down his back and collecting in a pool at the top of his belt, he saw her head droop slightly, and, like an overwound spring, he exploded across the opening. But he didn't move fast enough.

The lasher struck at him with all her fury, her tongue lashing, lashing. "You can just put that golf stick away, Mabry Russell! You're not going anywhere until you clean the garage. I have been after you for months to do something about that God-awful mess. Do you want <u>me</u> to do it? Do you want <u>me</u> to clean it up, on top of everything else I have to do around here? Do you?"

"Aunt Tillie's Pendant"

A FEW YEARS BACK I inherited a most unusual piece of "jewelry" from my mother. It was her Aunt Tillie's pendant. My mother's sister, Tillie, was married to an evangelist Southern Baptist preacher by the name of Yelveton O'Rourke. Uncle Yel was devoted to personally converting all of Africa to Baptist Christianity. He married Aunt Tillie in 1919, shortly after he returned from Africa at the end of WWI. He had served as chaplain to an American military unit sent to Tanzania to combat a German unit operating out of what was then a German colony.

Much to his chagrin he discovered, while serving there, that very few of the native peoples were devout Christians, and none of them were Southern Baptists. Convinced that salvation for the poor, benighted "darkies" depended on their conversion to his brand of Christianity, he took Tillie to Africa shortly after their honeymoon, with the financial support of five churches in the south Georgia county where he grew up. Tillie didn't share Yel's enthusiasm for evangelism, but as a dutiful wife she went peacefully.

It took her several months to get used to the heat and bugs and snakes and rain and mud and nakedness everywhere she turned, but Yel loved the life from day one since he was already used to it, and he felt that converting the natives was truly his calling. He had absolutely no respect whatsoever for their traditional customs and rituals and immediately forbade the observation of all of them.

Being naturally polite to foreigners, the Gobosi people tolerated his behavior, periodically admonishing him gently not to push them so hard. Chief Walakambusi even met with him on several occasions to explain how he (Yel) must not be disrespectful to him, his host. But such admonishments went unheeded because Yel was convinced that God was working through him.

Finally, when Yel demanded that the adults have just one sexual partner, and cover their nakedness, and not eat raw snake entrails, the chief could take it no more and ordered Yel be confined in an empty animal cage. Upon paying him a visit there the chief asked him if he now understood the error of his ways. Yel indignantly shouted that God will punish him and all his people for transgressions against Rev. O'Rourke, God's emissary.

Still not sure what this "God" is all about, but not wanting to take any chances, the chief returned to his quarters and planned a strategy for avoiding God's wrath. He decided to disguise Yel so that God wouldn't recognize him as his emissary. In the meantime, Tillie was of course worried about her husband and what might happen to him, but was greatly relieved when the chief came to her hut smiling broadly. He told her he was returning her husband to his home, turned to an aide standing behind him holding a bowl, took an object from the bowl, and handed it to Tillie, who promptly fainted. It was Yel's head, shrunk to the size of a crabapple.

When she left the country a few weeks later, under the care of a Belgian physician from a nearby city, Yel's head traveled with her back to Georgia. Upon arriving home she was institutionalized in the Milledgeville asylum for several years. Although released in 1928 as reasonably cured, Tillie never again was "right in the head" and one day she found the head in a box in the attic and, attaching it to a necklace of jade stones she had bought at an African bazaar, she made a pendant necklace.

For the rest of her life she could be seen walking the streets of the town wearing the grotesque "jewelry." The townspeople learned to ignore it, but once in a while she would discover someone staring in horrified fascination at the brown, shriveled object resting on her breast. She would just remark sweetly, "That's my husband, Reverend Yelveton O'Rourke. As you can see, I keep him close to my heart."

"A Fond Farewell to Frank N. Stein"

IT IS WITH DEEP SADNESS that I bid farewell to our dear fiend friend, Frank. He was special to fiends and ghouls everywhere. As we all know, Frank was hard to pigeonhole. He was many people. He had Ralph's head, Louie's arms, Virginia's nose. Being with him was like being at a seance. It was so comforting to be among dearly departed human friends. The explosion that killed him—again—was tragic. Dr. Frankenstein forgot to teach him about the dangers of playing with matches while eating cabbage, but doc says not to worry. He'll be stitched back together in no time. But what about the replacement parts needed? The torso he got from Richard is beyond repair, so I hate losing Richard. And what about Virginia's lovely, delicate nose? Was that obliterated in the blast?

Oops! I apologize for getting off track. Despite all that, Frankie was a great pal. He was so thoughtful. Last week at his dinner party for Wolf Man's nephew, who was recently recruited to play for the Bulldogs, I complimented him on his Human Blood Pudding. The very next night he emailed me the recipe.

And as most of you know, I wouldn't even be here if it weren't for Frankie. He's the one who came to my coffin in the basement of the state capitol and pulled the wooden stake out of my heart. His story about that is hilarious. He had heard about my misfortune but didn't know how to get past all the government workers and legislators on the main floor. His original plan was to break in at night, but then he learned that the stake can only be removed during the daylight hours when vampires are dormant.

So he dreamed up a scheme to make himself welcome. He put on a polyester suit and patent leather shoes and plastered a big grin on his face. With hundred dollar bills sticking out of every pocket, he strolled down the main hallway. He said he tried to imitate John Travolta's famous walk down the sidewalk in "Saturday Night Fever." The clerks and secretaries looked disgusted and afraid, but the legislators rushed over to shake his hand and invite him to stop by their offices. He assured them he would, and excused himself to go the bathroom. A little while later he peeked out of the bathroom door and saw the coast was clear, so he slipped into the basement and freed me.

Boy, was it good to get that stake out of my heart. You can't imagine what it's like to spend decades having a strong urge to get out of my coffin at nightfall but being pinned to the bottom of the casket. It was especially bad when a full moon appeared in the basement window. It was on moonlit nights that the humans could easily see me coming after them. Seeing their terrified faces was fabulous fun. Now, thanks to our dear scattered Frankie, I'm having more fun than I've had in centuries. This current crop of legislators are very eager to retain me as a consultant on bloodsucking, and they provide me with plenty of plump taxpayers as payment. I don't have to work nearly as hard as I used to, which is a darn good thing for a vampire who will soon be 570 years old.

Oh well, I'm rambling again, so I guess I better close. I raise my goblet of fresh blood to you, Frank N. Stein. You were several of a kind.

Your Fiendish Friend,
Χουντ Δραχυλα
Count Dracula, B.S. (Blood Sucker)

"Child of the Wind"

BRUNO HEARD THE FRONT DOOR knocker banging and settled back on his haunches close by. He didn't like having door duty, but it's what his humans expected of him, a "mostly Lab." His real name was Child of the Wind, given to him by his mother as she was biting the umbilical cord that connected him to her.

His mother, Soft Muzzle, had done the same for all the pups in her three litters. She knew that as soon as the pup became an independent creature it needed a name. This helped establish its independence and identity. In his case a puff of cool air had caressed her soft muzzle as she was biting the cord and she immediately understood his special significance.

As for door duty, he couldn't care less what creature did or did not approach. He was interested only in the auras associated with them, and the connection of theirs to his and the rest of the auras in the network. Humans burbled about the wonders of something they call the Internet. But he couldn't understand their fascination with such a primitive aura.

A sudden sharp clap of the door knocker brought him back to his duties. A human claiming to understand the spirit world was out there and needed to be sent away. The visitor had indigestion—a little burping—ate a meat sandwich hurriedly a few minutes before—getting impatient—feeling anger. Bruno decided to imitate a St. Bernard but his voice failed him. It came out like a hoarse yawp but with the desired effect. The human told himself that the dog was dangerous and he should share his knowledge of the spirit world elsewhere.

After the aura of the visitor had dissipated, Bruno walked over to the throw rug in front of the fireplace, turned around three times and lay down with his heavy head resting between his outstretched paws. The afternoon sun slanted through the window. He greeted the sunlight and thanked it for warming his coarse, dark brown fur. It also soothed his joints, which had begun to ache a little in recent years.

As he lay there, on the threshold of sleep, he thought of other humans he had known in his life. Soft Muzzle's human Curly Hair had crawled under the house and taken him and his brothers and sisters from their bed of rags. At the time, his eyes still closed, Child of the Wind didn't know the human had curly hair, but his manner was gentle, so Child liked him. When Child's eyes finally opened, the first thing he saw were his squirming siblings on the towels in the cardboard box. The next thing he saw was Curly Hair reaching for him.

A few weeks later, "Bruno" was a stout, alert puppy who enjoyed romping with the other puppies. One day a new human, Dark Eyes, picked him up, nuzzled his pink nose and commented on his sweet puppy breath. A little while later Bruno was moving in this large, loud force. It resembled a thundercloud rolling across the sky except that it conveyed motion and had a complex of smells. He was in a box behind Dark Eyes and Gas Smell, who were seated next to each other on the other side of a brown wall. He could see only their shoulders and heads. Periodically Dark Eyes would turn and smile at him, much like Curly Hair did. He rather liked the rocking motion of the "cloud" and fell asleep as they moved along.

When they stopped, Dark Eyes picked him up and walked toward two smaller humans. Bouncing Hair giggled and jumped up and down, her arms reaching toward Bruno. Scab Arm showed less enthusiasm but was obviously very happy to see him. The puppy quickly adapted to living with his humans. They were kind, even loving, to him and provided for his every need. All they asked in return was his affection and a little guard duty. He grew quite fond of them despite their grievous inability to read auras.

Now, ten years later, he was content and comfortable in the bosom of Dark Eye's family. Bouncing Hair was a teenager with many outside interests, but her extensive contact with the outside world taught her nothing about auras. For that matter, Gas Smell had many, many years of experience out in the world but was even more ignorant than Bouncing Hair. Bruno had come to understand long before that the older humans get the less connected they are to the auras of the world. Their "knowledge" promoted ignorance. Scab Arm was a philosophy major in his senior year at State, but he was nevertheless as ignorant as the other humans.

Now in the twilight of his life, Bruno spent increasingly more time on the throw rug, fully domesticated to "petdom." But every once in a while his canine self would awaken and he would raise his massive head, ears erect. Once again he was Child of the Wind, and Soft Muzzle and all his ancestors before her would speak to him, reminding him of his connection to the auras of the world and all they had to teach.

"Floodtime"

THE LOW RUMBLING THUNDER IN the distance told Bernice that Prescott County was not out of danger yet. Working day and night in shifts, every able bodied citizen filled and stacked sandbags to keep the roiling, boiling waters at bay.

Wearing an apron over jeans, and a badly faded denim shirt, Bernice sat heavily in the rocking chair on the porch of her little farm house and looked out across her pasture toward Bold River, which bordered her twenty acres. It looked more like Bold Lake now that it had overflowed its banks. Her cattle—Solomon and his three wives—had been moved to higher ground, and she had harvested all of the corn, beans, carrots and peppers she could, in advance of the rising water.

Now helpless to do anything else, she brushed aside her wet, grey hair and pulled out the tattered cuff hanky from her denim sleeve. She wiped the sweat from her eyes and then used the opposite corner of the cloth to clean her bifocals for a better look at the lake, shimmering in the distance like a mirage, in the pasture, just below the wrought-iron fence which surrounded the family graveyard.

Fighting the flood had been scary but exciting. How perfunctory, how routine her life had become as a widowed schoolteacher. In years past there had been men friends, her teaching career, her charity work, her anti-war activities during Vietnam and, of course, the farm. All that was left now was the farm . . . and her memories.

The flooded pasture took her back to the spring of 1942 when she and her new husband Rafe Henry had sat on this same porch—in better condition then—and watched the lake form. Back then the new, bright white swing had been used often. Now the paint on the slats was chipped and faded, and the wood was so brittle that only Sadie the cat trusted it to bear her weight.

The showers that April had been especially heavy, as they sat together, on the swing, without speaking, without swinging, and gazed out at the lake, which mirrored the brooding clouds and the somber mood of the couple. Rafe had been called to duty and was to report to Parris Island,

South Carolina the following Tuesday. While they stared at the water, they listened to the popular new apple tree song as it drifted through the window from the Philco in the parlor. She now found herself mouthing those old lyrics . . . "Don't sit under the apple tree . . . with anyone else but me . . . anyone else but me . . . anyone else but me." Even though she prided herself for not being sentimental, she felt tears tracing the wrinkles of her face.

"Bern, you won't sit under an apple tree with Randy Stokes while I'm gone, will ya?" Even before Rafe would smile, his light blue eyes would "crinkle" and betray his amusement.

When the itching of her scalp broke her reverie, Bernice shifted her weight in the rocking chair. Unconsciously she lifted the grey wig from her bald head and gingerly scratched the offending spot. The chemotherapy had done a great job of making her bald but not much to slow the spread of her breast cancer. But it didn't matter. She had her good days and her bad days, and this was a good one: the pain wasn't too bad, and she couldn't do any farm work, so she would just spend some time with "my men," in a flood of memories.

When she was twenty-two, newly graduated from college and recently married, her hair was luxuriant, dark red, and it reached down to the middle of her firm, narrow back. Her husband—she was pleased to recall—had loved to spread it artfully over the pillow before they made love. Now old, fat and bald, she chuckled when she remembered how all the girls and women had worn their long hair hanging down over one eye, in the Veronica Lake style.

"Lake?" She saw that a momentary break in the clouds had given the sun a chance to break through and bathe the lake in sunshine, making the surface sparkle with dancing light. As her spirits rose, she stopped rocking, reared back in her chair, straightened her shoulders, raised her chin, and looked off in the distance.

"Rafe, do you remember swimming in that river cove around the bend from the Pearsons' place? That rope swing on the sycamore tree was such fun. Must have rotted away by now. I'll never forget the day Pauline Dudley lost the top of her bathing suit when she hit the water. And the embarrassing remarks Roy Bedlow put in *The Parnassian*. I've still got that old high school yearbook, with Pauline's comments about the incident." Looking at all that water made Bernice aware of a need to urinate, but she was so content sitting there that she decided to wait.

The thought of urinating amused her and reminded her of Rafe, Jr. and those horses he loved so much. One of her strongest memories of those days with him at the stables was watching horses "pee." Whether stallion, gelding, filly or mare, they could let fly with a torrent of water that would splash outrageously in all directions. What she and Rafe, Jr. had found so amusing was the horses' grand indifference to their grossly bad manners. Now, every time she smelled ammonia, her thoughts traveled back to a horse in a stable stall and Junior brushing the horse, laughing with her.

How she loved the memory of standing on the porch, looking down the pasture to the tree line bordering the river, watching a twelve-year-old Junior ride his appaloosa, Apache, at full gallop, toward the river, swinging his cowboy hat, whooping as loudly as he could, his dark red hair tousled by the wind.

"Junior, I saw an appaloosa the other day over near Farley. Looked a lot like Apache, but his mane was cut short."

Reminiscing about Junior and his horses was very pleasant, but inevitably another memory would intrude: he is seventeen years old, working a summer job as a groom in Lexington. He is in the stall brushing a very large, dark chestnut three-year-old. A loud thunderclap startles the horse, and he bolts, crushing Junior against the wall of the stall. At first they thought he would be all right, but by the time they discovered the ruptured spleen, it was too late.

(Ring!)

"Hello?"

"Mrs. Henry?"

"Yes"

"This is Frank McBride at Sundown Stables . . . Junior's been in an accident . . . ."

She remembered how Frank's voice grew weaker as though he were rapidly moving away from her. And how the darkness narrowed her vision. Only by pressing a hand and a knee against the credenza had she avoided crumbling to the floor.

In an effort to dismiss the painful memory, she concentrated on the letters she and Rafe exchanged over the last months of 1942. Occasionally she would get one containing holes cut by the censor when Rafe would reveal more than he should have about his location and his activities. How appropriate, she had thought, that the government put holes in her letters to match the holes in her life. Reaching for a well-worn cigar box at her feet, Bernice carefully lifted the barely attached lid and drew out a severely creased sheet of paper, yellow with age. She carefully unfolded it and slowly raised it up in front of her face and, through the holes created by the censor of her life, she peered out at the troubled waters and thought of all the tears she had shed.

"Rafe, I want to tell you about the flood. Roscoe Sedgfield's place is completely under water I hear. You remember Roscoe. You went to high school with him. He's also one of the men—I told you this I know—I dated just after the war. But, as you know, I just couldn't get used to the idea of another man on your family farm, especially with your Ma still living there and all. And I had my teaching career, which took a lot of my time. Having a stepfather for Junior also didn't sit right with me. One thing led to another. The years flew by. I got set in my ways . . . ."

In those turbulent last months of 1942, she had written letters, long, newsy epistles nearly every day, and weeded her Victory Garden, and gathered newspapers and tin cans for the war effort. She had also helped with War Bond drives and worked at the Canteen on weekends. The reason she had so much free time was that she had left her teaching job to have a baby. And being pregnant, she found, gave her enormous energy. She glowed with health and sparkled with vitality . . . . So different from now when she felt diseased and drained.

Then came the cruelest, blackest day of her life. She had been busy stirring a boiler of fudge to take to the Canteen when she heard a knock on the door. Standing there was a Western Union boy, his hat tucked under his arm. The rest is a nightmarish blur: some God-forsaken place called Guadalcanal . . . a sniper . . . . Just the day before she had bought some baby things, and a stack of diapers was sitting on the telephone stand next to the front door. After the boy left, she grabbed the top diaper, buried her face in it, collapsed onto the sofa, and cried in wrenching, wailing sobs, completely lost in time until she noticed that the parlor had grown so dim it was almost dark. The air was dense with the pungency of burnt fudge. From that day on she could not stand the sight or smell of fudge.

Both Rafe and Rafe, Jr. were buried in the family graveyard. Despite her poor eyesight, Bernice could still see the headstones of her two loved ones among the others. She held up the censored letter and peered through one of the holes so that all she could see were the two graves and the empty space between them, waiting for her. Then she lowered the letter to her lap and looked at all the holes in the page. Giant, gaping holes.

As Bernice contemplated the emptiness of her life, all of the residents within two miles of Bold River Dam were moving to higher ground, as much more rain was expected, and water was cresting the dam. Sandbag levees were abandoned, and the weary farmers and merchants and doctors and teachers and children had given up trying to control nature and were heading for higher ground.

"Rafe? Junior? Sheriff Dobbs called to tell me to get to higher ground as soon as I can, and I told him I was going to stay with my cousin in Farley so he wouldn't worry about me." But Bernice had decided to head for the highest ground of all. She was going to stay put, and if the dam broke and "drowned" her loved ones, then it could just drown her, too. She was sick, she was tired, and she was anxious for them to be the family they never were. So she sat there, tenderly holding the fragile letter, rocking and waiting, while the threat of more rain rumbled in the distant, darkening sky.

"The Scars on Judy Weiss"
(mostly fiction)

IN THE SUMMERS OF MY Alabama childhood, I wore nothing but short pants. No shirt, no shoes, no underpants. Upon waking up in the morning I could be outside playing in less than a minute, unless Mama caught me and made me wash my face and brush my teeth. My hair was too short to comb. My buddies and I played hard and got many scratches and cuts. Unless it was an ugly wound, parents didn't take their children to get sewn up. By age nine or ten each of us had an impressive display of scars on our exposed skin.

As young adolescents, we began wearing T-shirts and sneakers. This meant less skin was exposed, so when one of us took off his shirt we might see a scar we hadn't seen before and ask about it. Eventually scar stories became a pastime for us. It didn't matter if we got truth or fiction, as long as the story entertained us. Sometimes we would ask about a scar we already knew about, to see if the next accident report might be better.

I remember one afternoon in June of 1952. We were crossing the Standard Club golf course on our way back from Meader's Creek, and we stopped at a clump of wild plum trees at the edge of the rough. After filling our pockets with fruit we sat in a circle on a nearby tee box in the shade of a mock orange tree. Like the others I was flushed and sweaty. My brown hair was dark and damp and stuck to my forehead.

While we were enjoying the plums and the shade, "Snake" Ferguson spoke up. "Green, tell us how you got that ugly scar on your ugly head." Then he spat a plum stone at me. Apparently my reddened skin had made the white, crooked scar, just above my eyebrows, much more visible. After spitting a stone back at him, I considered telling a whopper worthy of such a handsome scar but decided that something close to the truth was sufficient.

"When I was two my brothers and sisters took me up in the tree house in the chinaberry tree in our backfield. I remember leaning over the railing to get a better look at a white dog on the ground. I fell out and landed on my head."

"That explains a lot about you, Green," said Donald Jackson, the most bookish of the gang. Then he took a small bite of a fat yellow plum and the juice squirted on his glasses.

"How far did you fall?" asked Snake.

"Twenty or thirty feet. Anyway, my sister Margie says that a big flap of skin on my forehead was laying over my eyes and nose and blood was pouring down my face and on my T-shirt. My brother Buddy grabbed me up and took me in the house. They put me in the bathtub and the water was red as blood. I didn't think that was a good time to be gettin' a bath. Then they took me to the hospital and they sewed back that flap of skin with fifty stitches."

After a moment of quiet reflection, Donald and Richie Matthews came over to get a closer look at what could have required fifty stitches. On his way back to his spot, Richie stopped and said, "I got a doozy of a scar on my crotch!" As he said this he unbuckled his belt. Judy raised her leg and swung it like a club, striking him behind the knee. His leg buckled but he regained his balance and strolled back to his spot on the tee box, laughing while buckling his belt.

Her action surprised me. Judy was a complete tomboy, just one of the gang. She had been a Panther from the day we started our club a couple of years earlier. She could do anything we could, and she could whip Donald in a wrestling match. One day when Snake called her "Jew-dee" when she wouldn't eat a pork hotdog, she jumped up and grabbed him around the neck and pulled him to the ground. For a while there it looked like she might win, but he got back on his feet, dragging her with him, and then threw her off.

We listened to a few more scar stories. Donald explained a small scar on his leg. He tore his calf muscle on a rusty barbed wire fence while trying to get away from a black bull (or so he said). He was crossing the bull's pasture and forgot he was wearing a red shirt. He got stitches and a tetanus shot. Snake parted his hair to show an ugly, two-inch red scar he got while attempting a one and a half dive off the city pool diving board. He said he kept his towel pressed on the wound until he got home. There was so much blood on the towel his mother had to throw it away. After the bleeding stopped, his mother put some iodine on the wound and left it open. Judy told about a scar on her right knee that she got at age three. She was running up the front steps of her synagogue when she tripped and fell. She placed both hands on her shin and pulled up her knee so we could all get a close look at the scar.

I don't know about the rest of the boys, but after her feminine reaction to Richie's behavior, my eyes wandered away from her knee. For the rest of that afternoon, wherever we went and whatever we did, Judy was in the middle of it. But for me it wasn't the same old Judy.

A week later I saw her at Pop's popcorn stand, and she told me she would be celebrating something called a bat mitzvah in a couple of weeks. She explained how that ancient Jewish ceremony celebrated a Jewish girl becoming a woman. After hearing that, I noticed things about her I had never seen before: a sheen in her black hair, a lilt in her voice, a shine in her eyes. Two weeks earlier she had been one of the boys. Now she was a woman. She had skipped being a girl.

I would turn fourteen in July and Judy had turned thirteen two months before. We were sitting on the white wooden bench alongside Pop's stand. The seat and back of the bench were marred by dozens of pocketknife gouges proclaiming the love of AH for ER and TM for WD and AL for PD and so on. I felt an urge to take out my pocketknife, but I couldn't see how she could love me. I was skinny and short—no taller than she. And barely pubescent.

When we parted she invited me to come up to the clubhouse the next day for a rehearsal for her ceremony. I had forgotten that the Weisses were members of the country club. Our house lot backed up to the golf course, so it was only a short walk up the hill, over a couple of fairways, to the clubhouse.

When I entered the cavernous banquet hall, I saw Mrs. Weiss and a few other ladies I didn't know. But I barely noticed them because my field of vision was overwhelmed by the sight of Judy in pink shorts and a white blouse hanging outside her shorts but tied in the front. She had on leather sandals, and her hair was brushed back in the Ava Gardner style. She wore a hint of a pinkish lipstick that matched her shorts. She looked nothing like the Judy I knew. She looked like an older woman.

After we chatted for a while, she told me her mother wouldn't need her for a while and asked if I would like to take a walk. I was stunned.

I could think of absolutely nothing I would rather do than take a walk with her.

We strolled along one of the fairways. She didn't just plod along like she normally did when out with the Panthers. She strolled casually and swung her hips a little bit. She was laughing, teasing me, occasionally stooping to pick up a dandelion or a blade of Johnson grass. At one point she grabbed a buttercup and smeared the yellow pollen on my nose.

I was not only smeared. I was smitten. During the previous school year I had been told a couple of times that a girl in my class "liked" me. My reaction had been, "So what?!" This was different. Those were girls. This was a woman.

After about ten minutes we began to sweat a little. Judy suggested we duck into a clearing in the middle of a nearby privet hedge thicket to get some water and shade. The golf course grounds crew had placed a spigot in the clearing for the hoses they used for watering the fairways and greens. We took a refreshing drink from the spigot then sat on the cool ground in the muted light under the privet canopy.

We talked about the Panthers, and I gathered that she would be leaving us soon. We talked about school and the YMCA party coming up, and about our families. I didn't have much to tell about mine. Janice would be married in the fall, my other two sisters were married, my brother Richard was playing Little League, my brother James was in the Navy, and Buddy had just graduated from medical school. Following graduation he had been inducted into the Army and was on his way to Germany.

My mention of Germany changed Judy's mood. Her bubbly, almost flirtatious demeanor disappeared. She told me about her aunts, uncles and cousins who had been sent to concentration camps and were never heard from again. Her mother's sister, Sophie, an unmarried librarian in Rotterdam, had managed to secure the necessary papers to get out of Holland and into England.

With difficulty she told me about her father's brother Morris who was freed from the Treblinka extermination camp by advancing Russian troops in May of 1945. While telling about Uncle Morris, her voice cracked, and a tear tumbled out of her eye and slid down her cheek. In that dim light I almost didn't see it, but the tear caught the light just as it rounded her cheekbone. I asked her what was wrong, and it took her several seconds before she could tell me how, according to her father,

her Uncle Morris suffered a severe personality change after surviving the camp. He was no longer the gentle, happy-go-lucky man he had been. For years after the war he went from job to job, none lasting more than a few weeks. Her father finally insisted that his brother come to America and stay with them for a while. Uncle Morris arrived when Judy was eleven.

One day he came into her room when he thought no one else was at home. They talked about school, and he teased her about boyfriends. His broken English made her giggle. Then he said, "You betta watch out on the boys. They like to feel girls." As he said that he grabbed her leg just above the knee. At first she thought he was just being playful. But when he slid his hand up and under the leg of her shorts, she screamed, slapped his hand and jumped backwards. When she did, his fingernails gouged out a chunk of flesh from her inner thigh.

While relaying this detail, she winced and pointed at a spot just below her crotch. She said her uncle was trying to calm her down when her father burst into the room and slapped him so hard he fell on the bed. A few days later they sent Uncle Morris back to Europe.

She said that blood from the scratch ran down her leg. About a year later, the first time she had a menstrual period, blood ran down her leg in the same way. When she saw the blood, she screamed, but luckily no one was home at the time. I had learned a little bit about menstruation from eavesdropping on my sisters and was very surprised she told me about her period. That information was much too personal and disturbing, especially coming from another Panther.

Feeling embarrassed I asked if we shouldn't be getting back, but she looked at her wristwatch and said they didn't need her for another half-hour. After an uncomfortable stretch of silence, she looked straight into my eyes. I was transfixed by her warm, black eyes under thick eyelashes. She asked if I would like to see the scar. As she spoke she slowly stood up. At first I couldn't understand what she was saying. When I did understand, I couldn't speak.

The leafy enclosure became stuffy. My breathing became labored. I became aroused. My eyes wandered up and down her legs, which had soft curves from ankle to hips. I saw fine hair on her lower legs. Her chest was rising and falling in sync with mine. I stood up and smelled an earthiness coming from her that was different from the smell of the humus beneath our feet.

Her hand moved to the bottom of the shorts and slowly pulled them up. At first she pulled just the shorts, but then went back to include her panties. Once I could see the scar, she asked if I would like to touch it.

Many years later I saw the movie *Gigi,* and when Louis Jordan discovers Leslie Caron has become a woman without him realizing it, I thought of Judy. Of course I thought of Judy. In just a few days she changed from Panther to girl to highly desirable woman. I will never forget the day I was wonderfully wounded by a special scar on Judy Weiss.